Britain in 2010

CAPSTONE

Professor Richard Scase

Professor Richard Scase is exclusively represented by SPEAKERS for BUSINESS, Europe's leading business speaker bureau. SfB works with blue-chip clients to secure the very best business speakers for corporate events in the UK, Europe and worldwide.

For further information contact:

SPEAKERS for BUSINESS
1–2 Pudding Lane
London EC3R 8AB
Tel: +44 (0)207 929 5559
Fax: +44 (0)207 929 5558
Email: info@sfb.co.uk
Website: http://www.sfb.co.uk

Britain in 2010 demonstrates . . . that information technology will increasingly pervade every aspect of life.

Carl Symon, Chief Executive, IBM

If you're reading this you're in luck. Because it's probable that you are a well-educated, techno-literate, commercially sussed citizen posed to benefit hugely in the world of 2010

Jon Leach, Partner, HCCL

The data here begins to provoke our imagination, to think the unthinkable, to create, innovate and to provide the bridges from exclusion to inclusion.

Heather Rabbatts, Former CEO, London Borough of Lambeth

Good scenarios should be plausible enough to draw you in, but then be powerful enough to make you re-perceive the world you live in. Richard Scase's book does just that. So give youself time to read it – there's plenty to think about in your future

Tom Kippenberger, Editor, The Antidote

Britain in 2010

The new business landscape

Richard Scase

CAPSTONE

Published on behalf of the Office of Science and Technology. Applications to reproduce Crown copyright protection material in this publication should be submitted in writing to HMSO, Copyright Unit, St Clements House, 2–16 Colegate, Norwich NR3 1BQ. Fax: 01693 72300 e-mail: copyright@hmso.gov.uk

The right of Richard Scase to be identified as the author of this work has been asserted by him in accordance with the Copyright, Designs and Patents Act 1988

The views expressed in this book should not be taken to represent those of the Office of Science and Technology, the Department of Trade and Industry or the Economic and Social Research Council

First published 2000
Reprinted 2001

Capstone Publishing Limited (A Wiley Company)
8 Newtec Place
Magdalen Road
Oxford OX4 1RE
United Kingdom
http://www.capstoneideas.com

British Library Cataloguing in Publication Data
A CIP catalogue record for this book is available from the British Library

ISBN 1-84112-100-2

Typeset by Forewords, Oxford

Contents

Preface

The purpose of this book is to 'raid' the future from a series of perspectives, most particularly from that of social science research.

However we look at it, there has never been a more compelling need to see what the social consequences will be in the future of decisions made now – actively or passively – on our lives. This is true at a personal, business or governmental level.

This book is one of the outcomes of the work carried out by the Foresight programme's Leisure and Learning Panel and came about because – as group of people from a wide variety of backgrounds – we found we shared a passionate concern to connect different kinds of thinking about the future.

Why is it, we asked, that technologists seem often to be compelled to build scenarios which lack real social context? Why is it that the social sciences seem largely silent about the future?

The answer to this in part of course is that it is difficult. Some people clearly do take the view that 'futurology' is a waste of time and that scenario building is a flawed and imprecise way of thinking.

However as people in business and education we thought that we ought to take a different kind of stance.

What happens if you slice the problem up a different way and say that the future will be made up of a heady mix of things which can be extrapolated, things which stay endlessly constant throughout history and things which are discontinuous and which cannot be predicted.

And what happens if you encourage groups who do not normally work consciously on the same 'future' agenda to stare at the same 'pictures'?

Even if we do not like some of what the voices have to say, we reasoned, at least the process of disagreement or panic or revulsion or broader debate could lead to an improved process of conscious decision making rather than blind, passive, technologically-led optimism.

We will have achieved our objective if at least some of what is written here provokes. Argue with the contents of this book by all means. Disagree with it. Laugh at it. Just do not ignore it altogether.

I am extremely grateful to Professor Richard Scase for writing this book, and to the Office of Science and Technology and the Economic and Social Research Council for their support and co-sponsorship.

I am also grateful to our many contributors for their pieces written in response to Richard's work which in their thoughtfulness and stimulating observations begin just the start of the debate

Barbara Beckett

Chair, Leisure and Learning Foresight Panel

Acknowledgements

This book has benefited from discussions with many colleagues on the Foresight Leisure and Learning Panel: fuller details about the Foresight Programme can be found at the end of the book.

Special thanks are due to Barbara Beckett (Chair of the Foresight Leisure and Learning Panel), John Ginarlis of the Computer Sciences Corporation and Tim Whitaker of the Economic and Social Research Council. Acknowledgement is also due to Dr Michael Moynagh of the Tomorrow Project, Dr Jonathan Scales of the University of Essex, Kim Wager of the Office of Science and Technology, and to Janice Webb for all her administrative support. But most importantly, thanks are due to Professor Jonathan Gershuny who, as Director for the Institute for Social and Economic Research at Essex University, has created a World Class database of longitudinal trends in British Society.

About the author

Professor Richard Scase is Europe's leading business forecaster of scenarios for the next century. Currently Professor of Organisational Behaviour at the University of Kent at Canterbury, he also lectures at universities across the world. He is a recognised authority on cutting-edge business issues ranging from the impact of demographic trends for future consumer markets to managing creativity, the impact of information and communication technologies to future patterns of work and employment trends. As a prolific writer and a regular broadcaster he has contributed widely to the debate on how future socio-economic and global trends are likely to affect business strategies.

Towards 2010: some general themes

- ▶ **The uncertain outcomes of technology**
- ▶ **The characteristics of 2010**
  - *Individuality*
- ▶ **The uncertain outcomes of new technology**
- ▶ **The characteristics of 2010**
  - *Individuality*
  - *Choice*
  - *Mobility*
  - *Identity*
  - *Independence*
  - *Anxiety and risk*
  - *Creativity*
  - *Globalisation*
  - *Information and communication technologies (ICTs)*
  - *Bio-technologies*
  - *Socio-economic inequalities*

Towards 2010: some general themes

As we move towards the millennium, a wave of books predicting the future appear. Some of these are deliberately provocative with the purpose of generating debate. Others are downright speculative with little in the form of substance or credibility.

More sensible, realistically-grounded approaches which construct a view of the future based on the analysis of current trends are needed. They offer the opportunity both to interpret and to extrapolate so that, on the basis of studied facts, a more reasoned, balanced and sensible view of the future can be constructed.

▶ The uncertain outcomes of new technology

Links between the past, present and future are always featured by continuities and changes. Clearly many predictions of how information and bio-technologies will transform society are exaggerated. Technologies may be forces for change but they are constrained by social, economic and business structures. The outcomes of technological development are always uncertain. Forty years ago, it would have been difficult to predict that the major impact of hover research has not been the development of land/water mass transport but the "flymo". Equally, probably few technologists working on the development of Concorde expected that it would be used for day trips to see Santa Claus in Finland rather than for mass supersonic transport over the Atlantic.

▶ The characteristics of 2010

The purpose of this book is to focus upon future trends from a non-technological perspective. In doing this, it:

▷ draws upon empirical research;
▷ focuses upon both continuities and discontinuities in the changing character of modern Britain;
▷ makes extrapolations on the basis of existing trends
▷ explores the interplay between technologies, values, cultures and social institutions.

Its purpose is to encourage debate. It describes major trends and how these are likely to affect industries, lifestyles and business markets. In summary, Britain in 2010 is likely to be characterised by:

Individuality

Traditional family forms will no longer be the "foundation" of society. More of the population will live alone in single person households. This trend will affect lifestyles and work patterns. It will also have consequences for health and welfare systems, housing and retailing.

Choice

With declining family obligations, individuals will exercise greater choices in terms of where and how they live and work. This will lead to a greater diversity of personal lifestyles. Traditional marketing categories based on income and age differences will no longer be relevant.

Mobility

Individuals will be more mobile in all spheres of life including work and employment, personal relations and residence. Future lifestyles will be based upon mobility rather than stability.

Identity

Personal identities will be more "fluid" as a result of increased mobility and the more transient and temporary nature of work, leisure and personal relations.

Independence

Individuals, freed from traditional obligations and enjoying greater mobility, will value their personal independence. This will lead to more self-centred, self-indulgent and hedonistic psychologies.

Anxiety and risk

Individuals, in a more unstructured and rootless society, will feel more insecure. They will experience greater uncertainties and see society as high risk and often threatening. Others will find this more exciting and challenging.

Creativity

A focus upon self-interest and individuality will encourage personal creativity. This will generate a more innovative society.

Some of the macro-trends that are likely to affect the future character of Britain include:

Globalisation

This will lead to an international division of labour with greater global segregation – the under-developed and developed economies; the Islamic and Christian societies; Russia, central Europe and Euroland – but also to the "specialisation" of national economies. In the world of the future, the challenge for Britain is to become a leading-edge, information economy.

Information and communication technologies (ICTs)

These will bring about the decline of traditional forms of organisation, ranging from large business corporations to government and the public sector. A key challenge will be to develop new social, economic and government institutions that can fully realise the capabilities of ICTs.

Bio-technologies

These have the potential to transform century-old patterns of reproduction and health as well as of psychological and physical health. The challenge will be to address the moral and ethical values associated with these.

Socio-economic inequalities

Britain is likely to be characterised by persisting social and economic inequalities with polarisations in cultural, educational and material living standards. These could constrain national creativity and the emergence of Britain as a knowledge economy.

After summarising some demographic changes, this book considers trends in work, employment and education. It then reviews changing lifestyles and consumption patterns and explores cities and communities of the future. It continues with a discussion of the changing role of politics and government. It is then concluded by some personal commentaries about these trends.

1

Living in the future: three scenarios

Living in the future: three scenarios

▶ Scenario 1: Rachel in 2010

The year is 2010 and Rachel is an advertising executive. She runs her own business and has clients throughout Europe. She started her own business after working for major companies based in New York, Sydney and Toronto. She graduated in 2003 with a degree in media studies and healthcare.

Unlike her parents who were students in the early 1980s, she did not go to university except for a couple of self-development and personal creativity courses. Instead, she studied from home while working part-time in a supermarket. Using the internet, she took a portfolio of courses, selected from some of the most prestigious universities in the world. Most universities operate as virtual organisations. If they have a residential component, it is for short-term "creativity programmes" where students have the opportunity to engage in face-to-face dialogue with tutors – rather like the Open University residential courses of the late 20th century. Rachel's tutors were the best in their field – leading-edge researchers who regarded their twice a year, four week teaching commitments as a chore and a distraction from research. But developments in information and communication technologies have ended the old fashioned researcher/teacher role. There are far fewer academics than in the early 1990s.

Rachel has established a wide network of friends through the internet and this gives her contacts so that she frequently travels cheaply around the world. As a student, she had an email directory of at least 2000 names located in 48 different countries. It was through this network of contacts that she was offered her first job in New York.

She found work much like being a student. Most of the time she worked from her flat in downtown New York. She only went to the office for strategic briefings, team meetings or to meet clients. Otherwise, all of her work was done on a network basis. She worked always on short-time assignments which is how business is generally conducted. No-one worked for the partnership for more than five or six years as they were expected then to move on.

She returned to London and with two others set up her own business. Her current plan is to work until her late fifties. At some point she will have a child. She is still uncertain whether she wants a boy or a girl. That is something she will discuss with her medical consultant. She would also need advice as to whether she should defer giving birth until her late forties or early fifties. The final decision will probably depend on how well the business does. At least bio-technologies allow her to choose, unlike her mother.

She is also undecided whether she should carry on living alone. She enjoys the excitement that independence gives her. At the same time it gives her greater choice in terms of the gene pool for her intended child. Some of her friends have decided to live with somebody and then have children. Often this has not worked out. The offspring have turned out to be less intelligent and not as attractive as could be hoped. By living alone, she could freely decide.

In any case, money is no problem. Her personal insurance plan covers the potential risks incorporated in her future plans, including unemployment and long life expectancy. She is paying fairly high premiums because of newly-introduced government requirements as well as the stipulations of insurance companies. The government insists that following the phasing out of state pensions (except for a minority of low earners) all others should take out compulsory personal pensions. Her premiums are particularly high because the insurance company calculated that, given her genetic background and very healthy lifestyle, she is likely to be retired for at least 30 years and to live until her late 80s.

Her life-style is, indeed, very healthy. Naturally, she is a vegetarian and works out regularly at the gym. She also takes time off from work on a regular, but unpredictable, basis for short break holidays. This is one of the great attractions of being self-employed and is probably the reason why more than 30 per cent of the labour force are now self-employed. It gives them greater personal independence, particularly now that ICTs allow them to work most of the time from their homes.

Rachel's insurance company insists that she has regular health checks. These are generally unnecessary since she has a number of self-monitoring devices that allow her to gauge her mental and physical state. By comparison with her mother's working experiences of the 1990s she feels she has less stress. She only shops for clothes. The basics are ordered on-line and delivered to her apartment. The secure storage containers for foodstore delivery are now common-place, particularly in the large cities where most single, professional people now choose to live. City life is very different from twenty years ago. Government initiatives in the 1990s are now bearing fruit. Urban decline has been reversed and the fear of crime reduced due to technologies which enable citizens to call police response centres directly. The tagging of those with criminal records is now also taken for granted. Crime in London is almost non-existent in the wealthy, single-person, inner city areas. The newly-elected Labour government, enjoying its fourth term of office in the 2008 general election, claimed this to be one of its major achievements. Sometimes Rachel does worry about the future. She enjoys the variety and mobility of her life. This is as apparent in her personal life as in her work. She feels in control. But sometimes she longs for the stability and the security of her childhood. Her parents have now been married for more than 30 years. This is uncommon for most couples. But it does make her think about the meaning of life and whether she really knows who she is and what she wants to be. Would religion or philosophy offer an answer?

▶ Scenario 2: Craig and Maria in 2010

Craig and Maria are both 34 years old and live in Rochdale with her two children. One of these is from a previous marriage, while the other was born during a one year relationship she had while a teenager. Craig has never been married but has lived with two other women. He also has two children as a result of these relationships but he rarely sees either of them.

Craig has been unemployed most of his life. He left school at sixteen with no qualifications. This was of no surprise to his teachers since he played truant for much of his last two years. His teachers were not particularly concerned about this since at that time, in the early-1990s, there was little pressure on schools to take much action. This was before stricter controls were introduced by the government in 1998 which were then strengthened in 2002. Teachers, now on performance-related reward systems, have truancy figures built into their personal as well as their school's performance indicators.

After leaving school, Craig was put on a number of welfare-to-work schemes but he rarely stayed for more than a few months in any of the jobs he was offered. Like most of his teenage friends, he lived in a transient world of work and welfare. Sometimes he would take on casual work in some of the local small businesses and be paid "out of the till". These were mainly in independently-owned fast food outlets or in different parts of the retailing, cleaning and service sectors.

While working in one of these jobs he was caught pilfering. After doing community work for this, he began a career of petty crime – theft of car radios, house break-ins for home computers, shoplifting, etc. He usually sold the stolen goods at local boot fairs and this gave him enough money to survive. Inevitably, he finally drifted into the "real business" – drug dealing.

By 2001, this was a huge industry in the greater Manchester area. It incorporated all income, age and gender groups. All attempts to tackle the drug problem in the late 1990s had failed. The distribution, purchase and sale of drugs is now recognised to be at the very heart of the lifestyles of the so-called "socially excluded" and is a key force in sustaining illegal entrepreneurship. It provides a means of economic survival for those who lack the skills to benefit from the growth of the information economy. This means the police adopt strategies of containment rather than attempt to eliminate the problem. But the heartlands of many urban areas are characterised by the existence of rival gangs who profit through protectionism and who, informally, maintain law and order.

The only link that Craig has with the formal economy is through Maria's jobs. These are usually part-time and consist of working shifts in local supermarkets. She feels that the pay is poor but this is compensated by the security of the job and the fact that the hours can accommodate her domestic commitments. She prefers working in the supermarket to her previous job in a customer services call centre. She had found that work particularly stressful. Her performance was tightly monitored and there was no opportunity for personal contact. The media often described these workplaces as the sweat shops of the Information Age. Most of these have now been phased out with staff working at consoles installed in their homes.

For people like Maria, life is not much different than twenty years earlier. Despite the government's attempts to portray Britain as a dynamic 21st century, information economy, the routines of her life are much the same as those of her mother. Craig does not bother much with the children and when in the house spends a lot of the time switching between the 400 TV channels that the local cable operator provides. Not only does Maria assume most of the responsibilities for the children, she also has to care for her elderly parents aged 64 and 76. Her father, self-employed for most of his life, failed to make sufficient pension contributions and so now has little in the form of income support, except for the basic state pension. This means that he and his wife are heavily dependent upon their daughter's care and support, particularly since both suffer from minor disabilities. In Maria's eyes, Rochdale seems to be full of older people and they all have health problems. She does not look forward to getting old. Still, life could be worse.

The area has a good public transport system and it is easy to get into the centre of Manchester. This is useful for work but also for Friday nights. For years, she and her female friends have gone out together – normally to various pubs before finishing the evening at a party. It was on one of these nights that she met a friend's brother who lives alone. Her current relationship is such that she is considering leaving Craig, taking the children, and moving in with him. Everybody seems to be splitting up these days. But she feels she has only one life to live and so she should take advantage of anything that is going. Her friend's brother has a fairly safe job and has kept away from drugs. In this day and age, you have to look after yourself, she feels. In any case, she has recently been beaten up twice by Craig when he has been drunk.

Teachers are concerned about Maria's children. They have little interest in school and cannot use the computers. They are among the few children that do not have access to PCs at home and this is affecting their performance in many of subject areas. They have been carefully monitored for any emotional and psychological problems since the school's information system put them in the "at risk" category. This is a shared database with the local health authority, social services and the police. Certainly, the drugs they have been prescribed to cope with what the teachers regard as hyper-activity and poor concentration have helped. The prescription of drugs is becoming more and more commonplace. Maria is worried about her children. She can see no future for them except a life of insecure, low paid jobs, petty crime and unstable relationships. She feels there is little chance they will be able to look after her in her old age. She sometimes hopes for a political party that would represent people like her and bring about some major changes in society.

▶ Scenario 3: Duncan and Kim in 2010

Duncan and Kim have lived together for twelve years. They met at Leicester University in the early 1990s and have now known each other for almost twenty years. They still debate whether or not they should get married but cannot see the point of it. There are no tax benefits and the legal and pension changes that were introduced in 2008 make it even less of an incentive.

Duncan is a self-employed tax adviser and Kim works in a central government department. Although Duncan is self-employed, he has been engaged by the same corporate client for the past seven years. He likes the freedom this affords him. Provided he completes his assignments on time and within budget, the attitude of his company is that he can do more or less as he likes. This is in sharp contrast to the situation when he began his career in the mid 1990s. Then, he was expected to commute into work every day into the centre of London. It was not until the first years of the new millennium that the company decided to make full use of the capabilities of the rapidly changing information and communication technologies and embarked on a drastic cost-cutting programme.

The programme resulted in closure of its large, high rental offices in the centre of London. This office was no longer required since all the employees could work from home. The company kept a small presence in the City mainly for client meetings and colleague brainstorming sessions. But the value of this facility has been queried as most face-to-face contact with customers is now conducted on their own premises. Equally, meetings with colleagues are becoming redundant as everyone is now familiar with using interactive video and voice ICTs.

The company has been able to claim tax rebates because of its implementation of a number of home working policies. The government introduced these in order to reduce the volume of commuting into London as part of its environmental and anti-pollution policies. Overall, these have been successful, reducing the daily number of journeys into the capital by more than 28 per cent since the year 2000. As far as Duncan's company is concerned, it has paid for the installation of broadband cable in all staff and core consultant homes. It also offers compensation for additional home costs such as heating and the maintenance of home-based workstations.

Duncan's work involves considerable travel, particularly in Euroland. The harmonisation of tax laws, corporate audits and fiscal regimes had led to a huge expansion of the company's business in mainland Europe. This is the reason that he and Kim have chosen to live in south east England. The ten times per hour journeys by Eurostar make it a good location. Even so, Duncan has recently noticed that his company's clients in Europe are now more likely to exchange data on an ongoing basis through shared ICT infrastructures and that less travel is now needed compared with five years ago.

Kim, as a government employee, enjoys part-time flexi-work. She does half of this at her London office and the other half at home. This is convenient for her as she is also studying for a higher degree with Harvard University. She is now on module 7, having completed courses with universities in Australia and the UK. A consortium of transnational universities offer courses on the internet and accredit her studies. Kim enjoys collaborating with other students in virtual seminar groups as this allows her to share experiences with students worldwide. She also enjoys the intensive face-to-face contact at the "personal creativity" summer schools that are held at different participating universities. She feels that she learns more and develops her personal knowledge far more effectively than when she was a student in the 1990s.

Duncan and Kim have only one child. He is ten years old. He attends the local secondary school where all the children are expected to have their own PCs. For the small number of underprivileged pupils there are scholarships enabling them to buy their own computers. PCs are now at the very core of the pupils' learning process. More time is spent working on projects at home and attendance at school is more flexible. In this particular education area, unlike those in the more deprived parts of the country, the school has become a learning resource centre with teachers able to work with pupils on an individual basis. In collaboration with parents, teachers develop personal learning portfolios, much of which pupils pursue at home.

The work styles of Duncan, Kim and their son means that the home is the centre of their working lives. Although modern technology has replaced many traditional household tasks, they still need to employ a cleaner on a weekly basis and to have a live-in au pair. They both work long hours but at home instead of in the office. Their large country house is full of the latest information and communication technology. Each room has a large flat screen, which allows all forms of data to be received and transmitted. There is no need to shop for the basics as these are ordered on-line and delivered to the secure and temperature-controlled service box attached to the side of their house.

The bathroom is a medical centre and incorporates a variety of equipment for monitoring personal health. This ranges from blood pressure levels to psychological states. Duncan and Kim organise their daily work routines according to this information. It is also important to feed the data into the household database because this is used by their insurance company to determine their premiums. In fact the company has recently proposed that this information should be fed directly into its own database. The company uses this information to predict life expectancy and, through its collaboration with a private healthcare provider, recommends treatment as well as preventative care regimes.

Kim and Duncan have a broad network of friends all over the world. Travelling to Australia and the United States is now a common feature of their holiday plans. They make use of their home-based video conferencing facilities to keep in touch with their geographically-dispersed friends. These same technologies also enable them to monitor, on a 24-hour basis, the health condition of Kim's mother who is now in her 70s and lives in Central Scotland. In fact, Kim orders on-line all of her mother's shopping needs which on a daily basis, are delivered by her local supermarket. This is much more convenient than having her live with them.

Each of these scenarios reflect emergent trends in British society. Greater individualism, personal mobility, individual freedom and choice, and the greater use of information and communication technologies. But they also reflect the continuing divisions of British society in which economic, educational, social and cultural inequalities persist. Each of the scenarios reflects sources of continuity as well as of discontinuity. The challenge is to identify, in various aspects of lifestyle, which of these will be the more powerful. This is the task of the following sections of this book.

2

Demographics, households and families

2

Demographics, households and families

- What changing demographics means for Britain
  - The baby boom years
  - The rise of one-person households
  - Changing household size
- An increase in people living alone
- Differences of lifestyle between single men and women
- The economic impact of more single people
- Marriage falls in popularity
- Inequality in the household continues
- The vital importance of parenting
- Some questions

Demographics, households and families

▶ **What changing demographics means for Britain**

A key force for change over the next ten years will be demographic.
It is well known that Britain has an ageing population. People are
generally less aware that there will be a large increase in the number
of single person households and of women who, because of their
earning capacity, can choose to live alone. Both trends will affect the

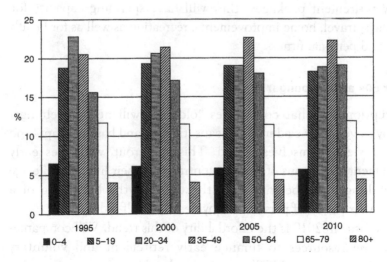

The ageing population: percentage in different age groups
Source: Government Actuary's mid-1994 based projections

21

demand for health and welfare services as well as patterns of leisure, consumption and life-style.

In the first decade of the 21st century, population will increase little. Britain's population, like that of many other European countries, will be static, possibly in decline. Birth rates will fall which, combined with increasing life expectancy, will lead to an ageing population. Over the next twenty years these demographic trends will bring a fall in the proportion of the population under 25 and a large increase in the middle-aged and the over 65s.

These population trends have important social and economic implications. At present, much advertising is targeted at the under 35s. The leisure and entertainment industries are orientated towards younger people. Newspapers and television companies are preoccupied with capturing a young audience for their products. In contrast, future growth opportunities are likely to arise from the life-styles and spending preferences of the middle-aged. A rising trend towards early retirement will create a growth in "time rich, cash rich" middle age consumers. With their company pensions and early retirement packages, they will have spending capacity for holidays, travel, home improvements, recreation as well as for health care and personal fitness.

Over 50s acting younger

Perceptions of what constitutes "old age" will need to change. Today's over 50s – clad in their jeans, trainers and baseball caps – no longer view themselves as old. This age group welcomes early retirement as a means of gaining control over their lives. Middle age is no longer the beginning of the end but the beginning of a thirty-year period of personal enjoyment and self-indulgence.

The issue in 2010 is the affordability of this trend. Will companies have the resources to finance early retirement and voluntary redundancy packages? Will government be able to finance a growing dependency ratio (the percentage of those non-active to those who are gainfully employed)? Or will it be necessary to encourage people to work into their sixties and even to extend the retirement age from 60/65 to 70? Older, experienced employees may even find that they are more attractive to organisations who become increasingly reluctant to lose those with corporate experience and valued intellectual capital.

The costs of caring for the very old

Growing numbers of very old people – those over the age of 75 – will create additional demands on state resources. Care for the very old is labour intensive and costly. The demand for medical services for the elderly will increase as life expectancy grows and more suffer from some form of disability. The increase in the very old could be a key driver for the application information and computer technologies (ICTs) in health care and welfare functions. The elderly will be encouraged to enjoy "independent lives", made possible by interactive, audio-visual monitoring technologies. The state is likely to become more selective in its provision of care for the very old.

A growing number of households

A further demographic trend is the growing number of households. Estimates suggest the need for between 4.4 and 5.5 million additional homes by 2015. This will be driven by increasing migration in Europe, longer life expectancy, more people choosing to live alone and a greater frequency of divorce and "split-ups" among those living together. Where will these new homes be built? In the 'global cluster' of the south of England? A significant proportion will have to be built in urban areas or the road system will grind to a halt.

▶ An increase in people living alone

About 80 per cent of household increase will be accounted for by

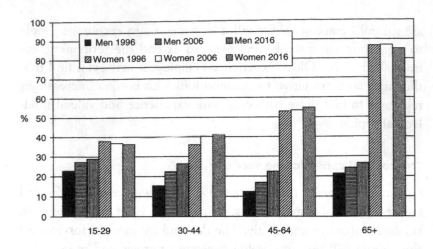

The growth of single person households (percentage of households comprising one person who is either never married, separated, widowed or divorced)

Source: Projections of Household in England to 2016, Department of Environment, 1995

persons who live alone. By 2010 single person households will become the predominant household type in Britain – accounting for almost 40 per cent of all households. The increase in single person households will be pronounced among those of younger middle-age. A high proportion of those in their twenties will continue to live alone before they engage in "live-in" partnerships. But more middle-age people will live alone not only because of divorce and break-ups but also from personal choice.

A growing number of women will live alone. Since the 1970s, an increasing proportion of women have obtained academic, professional and managerial qualifications. And more and more women have entered the medical, legal and management professions. Although women are still unlikely to obtain the most senior positions within their employing organisations, a growing percentage now have the earning capacity to finance their own mortgages and live independent lifestyles. This trend will continue and lead to the

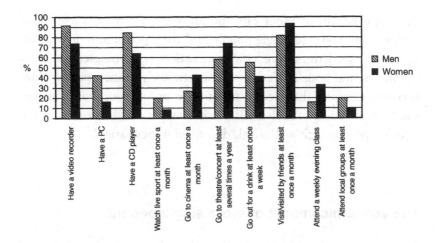

Lifestyles of single professional and managerial men and women aged 25–44 (percentages)
Source: ESRC British Household Panel Study 1998 (University of Essex)

emergence of gender-distinct lifestyles among men and women in their thirties and forties. Sociological studies suggest that women are likely to enjoy more intensive and broader social networks and to be more actively involved in leisure, recreation, education and cultural functions than single men. Singleness seems to make men sad.

▶ **Differences of lifestyle between single men and women**

If there are sharp differences in the spending and lifestyle patterns of single, middle age men and women this will have ramifications for corporate marketing and selling strategies. The outcome of this trend for consumer markets is likely to be significant. It will be a force for gender-based market segmentation and reduce the value of traditional income and occupational (socio-economic) categories for marketing and retailing products and services.

The growth of single person households is also likely to reinforce the rejuvenation of inner city, urban areas. Businesses associated with the life-styles of single people and their personal requirements will increase. Interactive communication technologies could be significant and housing developments are likely to incorporate video surveillance and other design features to protect occupants against the "fear of crime". Such built environments will be considered as vital for people such as Rachel, described in Scenario 1.

▶ The economic impact of more single people

The increase in single persons will lead to changes in the leisure and entertainment industries which at present focus upon "families" and couples. Introduction agencies are likely to flourish with service providers segmenting themselves as they focus upon specific age, occupation, and lifestyle categories.

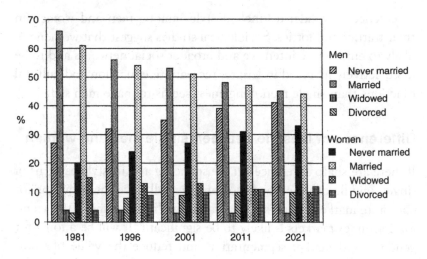

Population by sex and legal marital status, 1981–2021, England and Wales (as percentage of all adults)

Source: Government Actuary's Department 1996 population based projections (1999)

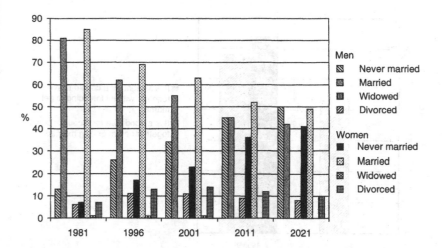

Population by sex and legal marital status, 1981–2021, England and Wales (as percentage of all adults age 30–44)

Source: Government Actuary's Department 1996 population based projections (1999)

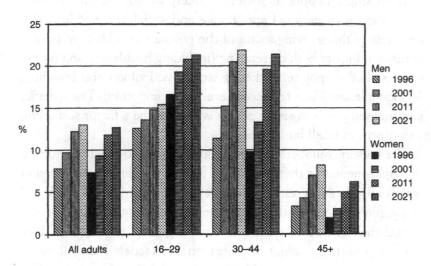

Cohabiting population by age, sex and marital status, 1996-2021 (%)

Derived from Government Actuary's Department 1996 population based projections (1999)

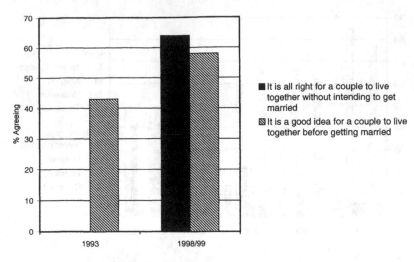

Attitudes towards cohabitation

Sources: 1998/99, British and European Social Attitudes Survey 1998/1999; 1993, British and European Social Attitudes Survey 1997/1998

More single people in society is likely to bring a greater pre-occupation with personal appearance and social acceptability. The demands of this growing sector of the population is likely to have a significant impact both on retailing (including health care and fitness centres) and corporate marketing strategies. Fashion and branding, for example, are likely to become even more important. The specific, personalised needs of single people is likely to be a factor sustaining the growth of small businesses.

The growing number of single persons is likely to affect the culture of employment. For them, work can be a central life interest around which all other interests and activities are subordinated. How will companies respond to these changing expectations? If single people regard their self-development as a major goal of employment, how will organisations adapt to meet these needs? The failure of employers to meet these could encourage single people to set up their own businesses. This is already the case for many highly educated women middle managers working in large organisations who hit the "glass ceiling" of promotion opportunity. If increasing numbers of men and women adopt such personal career strategies, the loss of talent to large companies could be even greater than it is today. On the other hand, this trend could be a major force in making the United Kingdom a more entrepreneurial economy.

▶ Marriage falls in popularity

Couple relationships are likely to continue to be transient for a growing percentage of the adult population with a high rate of break-up among those who cohabit and of divorce among those whoare married. The "churning" of partners will become even more pronounced.

The proportion of the male adult population who are married is predicted to fall from 56 per cent in 1996 to 48 per cent in 2011. In addition, the proportion of adults who have never married will increase from 32 per cent to 39 per cent in 2011 for males and from 24 per cent to 31 per cent for females. This will become particularly pronounced for those who are "middle age", i.e. people between the ages of 30 to 44.

While marriage will become less popular, Government Actuary projections suggest that the number of cohabiting couples could double over the next two decades, from 1.56 million in 1996 to about 3 million in 2021.

If 60 per cent of males cohabiting were over 30 years old in 1996, this will increase to 75 per cent by 2021. According to the Government Actuary's Department, "the net effect of the projected fall in marriage and rise in cohabitation is that the proportion of people living in couples will fall for most age groups, except for the elderly, over the next twenty-five years".

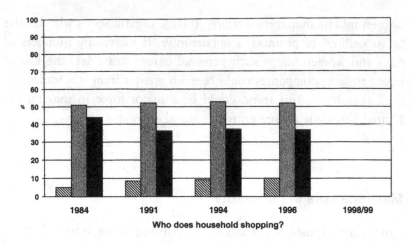

Who does household shopping?

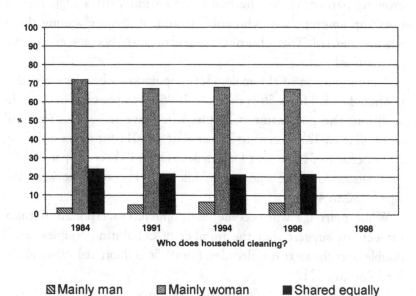

Who does household cleaning?

◊ Mainly man ▦ Mainly woman ■ Shared equally

Household division of labour

Sources: British Social Attitudes Survey: Social and Community Planning and Research 1984/1998; ESRC British Household Panel Study 1991–1996, University of Essex (1991-1996 figures based on woman's responses)

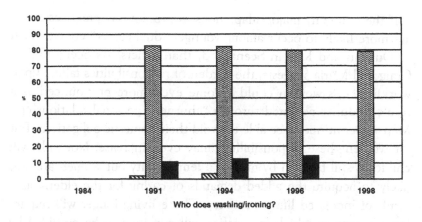

Who does washing/ironing?

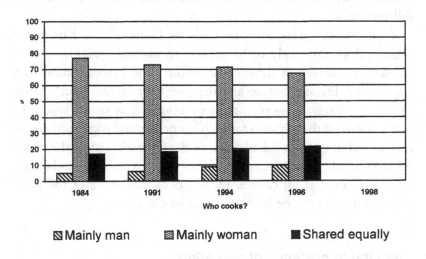

Who cooks?

▨ Mainly man   ▧ Mainly woman   ■ Shared equally

▶ Inequality in the household continues

For those living together, changes in the nature of gender roles are likely. In future, domestic duties may become more equally shared, but any shift in this direction should not be exaggerated. Research suggests that changes in the past have not been pronounced and are unlikely to be dramatic in future.

If there are any major adaptations in present-day practices, these are more likely to occur among younger "dual career" couples such as Duncan and Kim in Scenario 3, than others. As Scenario 2 of Craig and Maria suggests, the burden of responsibilities falling upon working class women could become even more pronounced as a result of duties acquired through "churned" personal relationships. Men will continue to be able to avoid their domestic obligations. But for women these responsibilities may even increase. Not only will childcare still be seen by men as a female duty but women are also likely to acquire the added demands of caring for the elderly as a result of increased life expectancy. Those living longer will require familial support which in practice will continue to be provided by daughters who themselves have children and work in part-time or full-time jobs.

With middle class couples, such as Duncan and Kim, their relationships are likely to be subject to mutual scrutiny as each assesses the nature of thheir relationship. The preoccupation with "authentic" life satisfaction and the quest for "meaningful" couple relations is likely to be even more pronounced in an age when the home becomes the location for both economic and social activity. In an ever changing world of work and of social relationships, the meaning of life will be focused upon the home, the family and couple relations. That is, of course, for the declining share of the adult population who will be living together as couples.

▶ **The vital importance of parenting**

In tomorrow's information economy, the quality of parenting will assume greater importance. In an economy based upon the production of innovative services, organisations that wish to compete in a global marketplace will need to nurture personal enterprise nnovative services, organisations that wish to compete in a global marketplace will need to nurture personal enterprise and creativity.

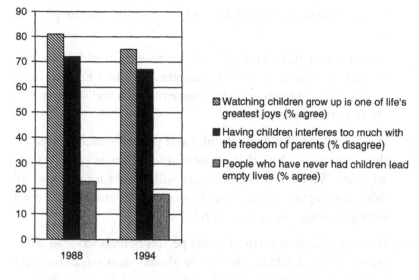

Attitudes towards children 1988-1996
Source: British and European Social Attitudes Survey 1998/1999

Children with parents such as Duncan and Kim will be advantaged in acquiring personal creative skills. Cultural differences between families of different socio-economic categories will have important consequences for the capabilities of their children to acquire the intellectual, social and technical capital necessary for personal achievement. An important challenge for government will be to "neutralise" home-based inequalities if Britain is to be a truly meritocratic society in which the creative talents of children can be realised.

▶ Some questions

▷ How will government respond to these changing demographic trends? To what extent will the welfare state need to become more focused in its provision of services and how far will it be necessary to compel individuals to save for their future personal care?

▷ How far can ICTs be exploited to provide health, care and welfare services at a lower per capita cost? In what directions should ICTs research and development focus and what are the priority areas for application?

▷ In what ways will the growth of single person households lead to the emergence of market opportunities for new products and services? Which economic sectors will benefit most? How will this demographic change affect corporate marketing and how will selling strategies need to respond?

▷ How far will the growth of single person households lead to the rejuvenation of urban areas? How should their needs be incorporated in town planning policies?

▷ How can the state develop and implement policies that will ameliorate the cultural differences between families of different socio-economic categories that affect the educatability and, hence, employment chances of children in an information age?

▷ How far would a return to "traditional family values" with a lower "churn rate" among partners have a devastating impact upon the economy through a reduced demand for housing and household goods?

3

Work, employment and occupations

- ▶ Britain's changing industrial and occupational structure
- ▶ The rise of "non-standard" employment
- ▶ An entrepreneurial economy
- ▶ Toward the virtual corporation
- ▶ The changing psychological contract
- ▶ More women break the glass ceiling
- ▶ Some questions

Work, employment and occupations

▶ **Britain's changing industrial and occupational structure**

Over the past twenty years the British economy has undergone major transformations. The decline of manufacturing and growth of service occupations is well documented. More people now work in Indian restaurants than in shipbuilding, steel manufacturing and in coal mining combined. There are currently three times as many public relations consultants as coal miners. This process is likely to continue as Britain becomes a predominantly service and information based economy.

In addition to these trends, major shifts in Britain's occupational

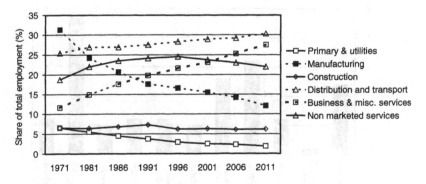

Changes in industrial structure
Source: 1971–2006 – Review of the Economy and Employment 1997/98, Institute for Employment Research. University of Warwick. (figures for 2011 based on linear regression of IER figures)

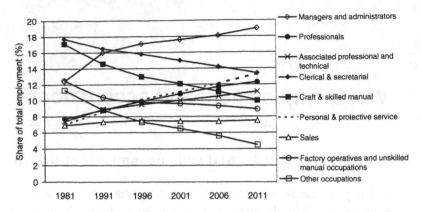

Changes in occupational structure
Source: 1981–2006 – Review of the Economy and Employment 1997/98, Institute for Employment Research. University of Warwick. (figures for 2011 based on linear regression of IER figures)

profile will also continue. Managerial and professional occupations will grow with a related decline in those engaged in skilled and semi-skilled manual tasks.

It would be too optimistic to assume that these changes will lead

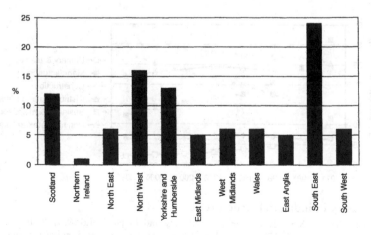

Percentage of UK call centre staff in different regions, 1997
Source: Guardian 2 June 1997

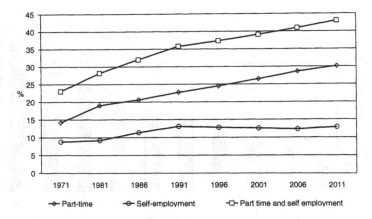

Growth of 'non-standard' employment as percentage share of all employment

Source: 1971–2006 – Review of the Economy and Employment 1997/98, Institute for Employment Research. University of Warwick. (figures for 2011 based on linear regression of IER figures)

to a more egalitarian society. Inherent in the growth of a service and information economy is the creation of jobs that are low paid, insecure and offer limited career opportunities. Changes in the retailing sector – the decline of traditional, independently-owned shops and the growth of supermarket chains – have created low paid and low skill jobs. The growing need for care assistants to look after an ageing population has led to the creation of part-time, low paid employment. Moreover, the growing use of ICTs is generating similar low paid jobs in call centres. These are expected to make up 5 per cent of the labour force by the year 2010. Low paid jobs could be the future of work for Maria's children.

▶ **The rise of "non-standard" employment**

By far the greatest number of jobs created over the next decade will take the form of "non-standard employment", i.e. part-time work, flexi-hours or self-employment.

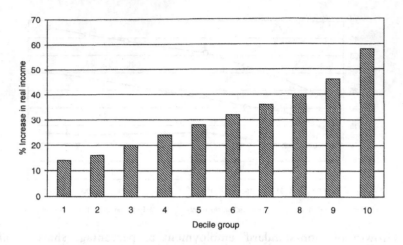

Changes in real income by decile group
Source: Department of Social Security 1999 (figures do not include the self-employed)

On one hand, these jobs may offer individuals the opportunity to earn wages in ways that are compatible with other commitments. In this sense, the future of work will offer personal liberation. But the more pessimistic view is that the future labour market will see the continuation of existing trends with the greater proportion of these low paid, non-routine jobs being undertaken by women, school leavers, students and older, pre-retired men. This will probably strengthen political pressures for a higher national minimum wage as well as for legislation to protect those who are particularly vulnerable. In Britain in 1999 there were approximately 2 million children actively employed on a part-time basis; a trend that is likely to continue with the casualisation of jobs in the retail, service and hotel and catering sectors of the economy.

▶ **An entrepreneurial economy**

A marked feature of the labour market over the next decade will be

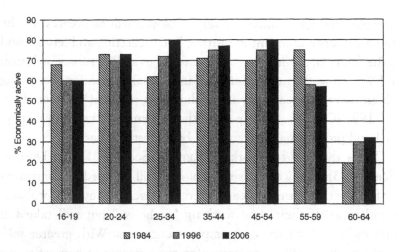

Economic activity rates for women by age

the growth of self-employment. In 1996, the self-employed made up 13 per cent of the labour market compared with 9 per cent in 1981. A reasonable projection is that this trend will continue but with significant differences across economic sectors. It is probable, for

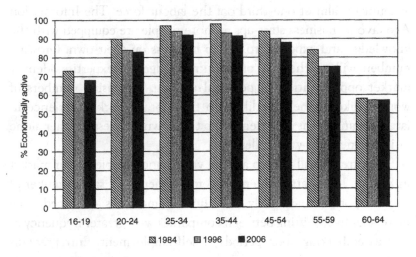

Economic activity rates for men by age

example, that the numbers of self-employed will be greatest in the media and entertainment industries, hotel, catering and leisure, and in the financial services sector. According to a 1999 survey by Bacon and Woodrow, the number of those in manual occupations becoming self-employed increased by more than 450 per cent between 1979 and 1998. Over the same period, the self-employed among managerial and professional workers grew by almost 300 per cent.

This is the world of work for Rachel (Scenario 1) and Duncan (Scenario 3). Many of the self-employed will be hired by companies on fixed-term, performance-related contracts. They will probably spend most of their time working "in house" but will take full responsibility for their own employment costs. With greater self-employment, it will be necessary for more people to have effective negotiation skills (know how to charge for their time) and be able to market their services to clients. They will be responsible for their own financial planning, including making sufficient provision for their pensions.

Small firms will be of growing importance. Small firms already make up 93 per cent of all enterprises in the European Union and account for almost one-third oof the labour force. The Information Age favours business start-ups as more people are equipped with the knowledge and expertise to set up business on their own. Growing numbers will, on the basis of their knowledge and expertise, identify market opportunities for personal trading. Increasing numbers of women, like Rachel, are likely to first obtain work experience in larger organisations and then set up their own businesses either alone or in partnerships with colleagues.

These trends will lead to a more varied and flexible labour market in Britain. Long-term careers and employment in a small number of large corporations are likely to decline as employees are forced to be more adaptive, shifting between companies with greater frequency as well as embarking upon periods of self-employment. Entrepreneurship will be more pronounced as companies continue to outsource

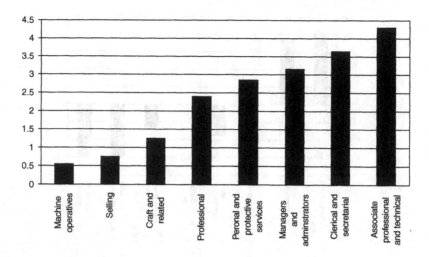

Percentage of employees and self-employed who work from home by occupation
Source: ONS, Labour Force Survey, 1999

many of their corporate functions. At the same time, a more self-reliant and "independent" culture among those who are technically and intellectualy expert will reinforce this trend. People's working lives will be more varied but shorter. Economic activity rates for both men and women over the age of 50 are likely to decline.

Rachel's work patterns will be determined by how she decides to manage and expand her business, the demand for her services by customers, and her preferred lifestyle. The workplaces of Duncan and Kim are likely to be very different. Both public and privatte sector organisations will be transformed in their operating practices by ICTs.

▶ Toward the virtual corporation

For service, professional and knowledge-based companies, innovation will be key to success in an increasingly global economy.

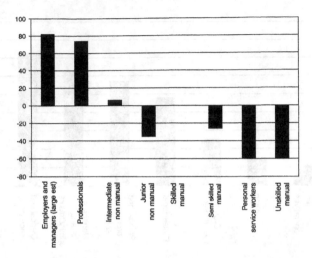

Percentage earning differentials – selected socio-economic groups
Source: Elias, P. and McKnight, J. (1998) Differentiating earnings by social class categories, Institute for Employment Research, University of Warwick. Based on Labour Force Survey 1993–1996

Hierarchical management structures that characterised traditional manufacturing companies and administrative organisations will be less evident. The management of intellectual capital will require skills that nurture employee creativity rather than worker compliance. This will demand more open corporate communication channels and the abolition of the "low trust" cultures that have characterised the predominant management style of 20th century British industry.

Many in-house corporate activities will be outsourced to different service providers. Managing these external relations within increasingly global-based supply chains will require skills in the planning and co-ordination of functions that will be heavily dependent upon information management through digital, broadband networks. Supply chains will be characterised by co-operative relations between companies through joint ventures, strategic alliances and partnerships. The development of global supply chains will mean that distance is no longer a factor in business. Small businesses located on the other side of the globe will not only be the suppliers of services but also operate as competitors. Small software companies located in Australia can obtain contracts with large companies in London, in competition with those based in the Home Counties. Equally, economies of scale will assume a diminishing importance as corporations become the "co-ordinators" of products produced within global-based supply chains.

The workplace of the professional, technical and expert workers will be designed according to rather different criteria than at present. With an increasing number of employees aand those on "retainer consultancies", such as Kim and Duncan, spending more of their time working from home, there will be less need for staff to have their own "exclusive" office accommodation.

Office space will be shared more efficiently, through such initiatives as "hot-desking", "hotelling" and the provision of a "public space" for meetings with colleagues and clients.

Organisational control will be exercised through the extremely effective "visibility factor". Individuals will have their own work stations (for the day) but will move into the highly visible central social areas when wishing to consult with colleagues or jointly solve work related problems. Workplaces of this design are already increasingly common in management consultancies, architectural practices and in media companies. This trend is likely to become more pronounced over the next decade as employee creativity is recognised as the key, perhaps only, asset that cannot be outsourced.

Working from home will be encouraged as companies recognise its cost-saving potential. Although home working will not abolish totally the need for office work, the growing capabilities of communication technologies are likely to shift the emphasiss towards the home. An estimated 40 to 50 per cent of the work activities of many managerial and professional activities are likely to be undertaken at home. The trend towards home working will probably be reinforced

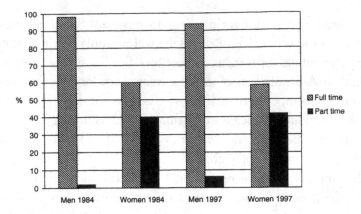

Percentage of permanent employees in full and part time jobs by sex
Source: Labour force Survey, ONS

by government policies to reduce traffic congestion, pollution and to encourage sustainable economic development. This trend is unlikely to affect those in low paid occupations such as check-out staff, cleaners, ticket collectors, receptionists etc. The impact of the Information Age is likely to reinforce a polarisation between the work and employment conditions of those in managerial and professional positions compared to those in service occupations.

▶ **The changing psychological contract**

In the workplace of the future, as experienced by Duncan and Kim, employees will have very different psychological expectations. Most employees will consider their organisational commitment to be temporary. They will have few expectations of long-term careers and will tend to regard employment contracts as essentially short-term negotiated arrangements. In such an environment, how can employee commitment and loyalty (which is vital to produce and service innovation) be fostered? How can intellectual property rights and other "intangible" assets be protected when information is

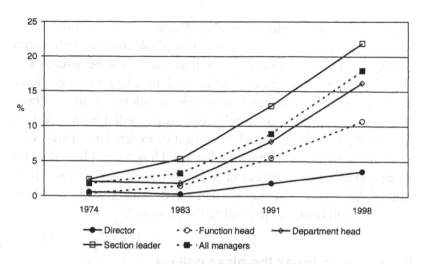

Percentage of managers who are women by responsibility level (percentages)

Source: National Management Salary Survey, Institute of Management and Remuneration Economics. Source: Social Focus on Women and Men 1998 ONS

shared through internet and extranet capabilities? Further, how can the split between work and leisure, office hours and home time be made when increasing amounts of corporate-related work is undertaken at home?

One answer is to organise work according to time and cost budgets, giving individuals the autonomy as to when, where and how they execute their tasks. But this solution would require a major change in management culture. While employee commitment is measured according to the length of hours spent in the office and while this is used as a criteria for salary increases and promotion, there will be few changes to patterns of work, including working from home. This could prove to be a greater barrier to change than overcoming the present-day limitations of ICTs.

Changes in the structure of work will have significant impact on individuals. Longer-term financial commitments such as house purchases will be more difficult to plan. Uncertainties and insecurities willl increase due to a greater frequency of job changes both within and between corporations. People will be required to be psychologically and emotionally more mobile, and to adapt more easily to working with a broader range of people in different work contexts. Emotional, creative and intellectual skills will become just as important as those of a purely technical or expert kind. Patterns of work are likely to be different for Rachel, Duncan and Kim than for Craig and Maria. The impact of ICTs will be greater for those whose work is "mobile" or "portable" than for the majority of the labour force who will continue to need "to go to work".

▶ More women break the glass ceiling

With the shift to flexible working, more women will be working in part-time jobs. But a growing number of women will also obtain senior management positions.

Women whose career progression continues to be thwarted by the glass ceiling will imitate Rachel and start up their own businesses. Indeed, women could easily become the major force of entrepreneurship in the UK economy over the next decade.

In this future world of work, it is difficult to be optimistic about the future of trade unions. Despite a recent small increase, membership is likely to decline as the employment relationship becomes more short-term and personalised. Their future role is likely to be one of friendly societies, offering advice, legal support and guidelines for employment practice. As a force for collective bargaining, their influence is likely to decline except in some areas of the public sector.

▶ Some questions

▷ What should be the responsibilities of national governments for ameliorating inequalities generated by the marketplace? Should this be through tax regimes or by more interventionist strategies? Is the United States or the European model more appropriate? Should the national minimum wage be but the first step for greater intervention in an economy characterised by the growth of "non-standard" jobs?

▷ How far will the growth in self-employment, part-time work and non-standard patterns of employment lead to old age poverty for those who fail to make adequate provision for their pensions? What are the likely outcomes for government policies?

▷ How can companies generate employee commitment when jobs are short-term and often outsourced? How can creativity be nurtured and intellectual property rights protected in virtual organisations?

▷ How far will the culture of management be the major barrier to realising the operational savings offered by using the full capabilities of information and communication technologies?

▷ To what extent will the creation of global supply chains reinforce the dependency of developing countries upon the operating strategies of multinational corporations rather than offering paths to economic independence?

▷ What skills will individuals need in order to cope with their more varied and changing working experiences? How will their attitudes towards savings and patterns of personal consumption be affected by these greater uncertainties?

▷ How could transport congestion be tackled with more active government policies encouraging public and private organizations to facilitate remote working?

4

Schools, universities and education

▶ A knowledge-based economy needs effective schools
▶ Schooling in an unequal society
▶ Universities face new demands
▶ A greater emphasis on life-long learning
▶ Some questions

Schools, universities and education

▶ **A knowledge-based economy needs effective schools**

The growing importance of Britain as an information-based society has consequences for its education system. The growth of the global economy with increasing regional specialisation and an international division of labour will have a major impact upon the country's competitive capabilities. A major requirement of the education system is that it can provide the intellectual capital upon which corporate creativity and innovation can be developed. It must also produce

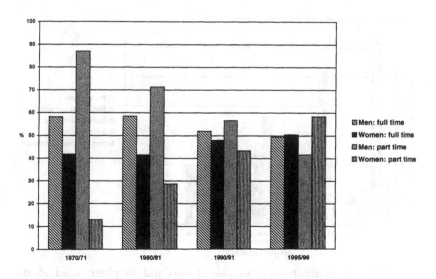

Enrolment in undergraduate higher education 1000's
Source: ONS Social Focus Women and Men 1998

effective inter-personal skills – a requirement which is driven by greater corporate understanding of the benefits which can result from effective teamworking. In addition, there is growing political demand for the educational system to instill notions of citizenship and ethical codes. All these demands are leading to greater and more complex pressures upon Britain's education system.

In the past, traditional gender roles, the greater permanence of personal relations and a more stable and orderly occupational structure enabled the education system to operate as a neatly structured system. Today, this is no longer possible. The increasing participation of women in the labour market places greater pressures on childcare, particularly the provision of pre-school nursery places. Formal or institutionalised education now begins at an earlier age.

The re-structuring of gender roles and the changing aspirations of women has led to the abolition in the overwhelming majority of schools of gender streaming. Girls now achieve higher average A-

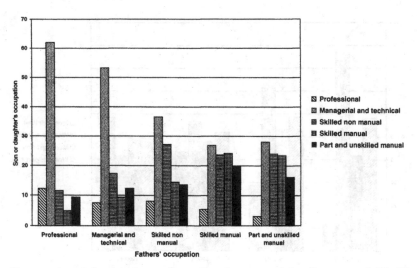

Occupational destinations of employed sons and daughters aged 35–65 by father's occupation (row percentages)

Source: ESRC British Household Panel Study 1998: University of Essex

level grades than boys and make up more than one-half of the university student population. Changes in the gender composition of universities is unlikely to change much more in the future. But it is likely that school curricula and university degrees will need to adapt to the changing identities and work roles of men and women.

In the past, the educational system reproduced the class structure. Children from manual working class backgrounds attended school until they were 16 and then entered the labour market. Children from white-collar homes continued at school until 18 before obtaining administrative jobs or going on to university. Teaching and learning regimes were structured according to these expected outcomes. While these patterns are less predictable today, a degree of inter-generational occupational inheritance still remains.

Despite continuities between the occupations of fathers and their children, differences are appearing. Greater movement between jobs classified in the same occupational categories now exists. There is also greater mobility by the same individuals in their life-long work patterns. These changes are shifting the emphasis of education as a childhood/teenage experience to life-long learning undertaken formally within institutions – such as colleges and universities – and informally at home and at work through the use of ICTs.

▶ Schooling in an unequal society

Nursery and primary education will continue to be a government priority as it clearly fulfils a key role in child socialisation and provides the foundations for effective inter-personal skills and personal creativity. Secondary education will continue to reflect the paradoxes of an unequal society. On one hand, it is a vehicle for a truly meritocratic society. On the other, the cultures and learning experiences which different schools offer reflect diverse socio-economic environments. The challenge for governments will be to

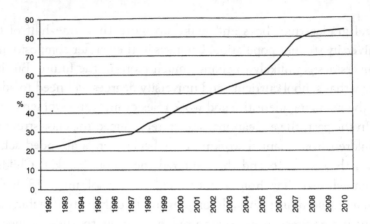

Percentage of houses with a PC

Source: 1992–1998 British Household Panel Study; 1999–2004 projections based on DTI projections for 2004; 2006–2010 extrapolations based on trends

break down the cultures of poverty which result in unequal educational opportunity.

The introduction of performance-related reward systems for teachers, intensive audits of school performance for league tables, and the management of schools by private sector service providers are all attempts to improve the quality of schooling. But it is unlikely that schools can do more than neutralise the impact of neighbourhood and home cultures upon children's educational achievement. Maria's children will still have the odds stacked against them. The reality for both present and future generations of children is that changes in the occupational structure will increase the need for check-out, call centre, and other low-paid staff. Schools may be a force for change – in shaping pupils' achievements and aspirations – but in a society where unequal opportunities persist.

Schools in wealthier areas will invest most heavily in information technology. It is these same schools that will attract sponsorship partnerships with corporations. If more private funding is attracted into the school system it is likely, with some exceptions, to reinforce and even exaggerate present inequalities in educational attainment. These inequalities could present a major obstacle to Britain becoming a competitive information economy. Already, some countries in the EU have the goal of giving each school child a personal computer – at primary, let alone secondary school level. When all children have access to PCs, the learning process can be transformed. With the use of ICTs, there can be greater interaction between home and school in the learning process – far greater than is possible through homework alone – with both parents and teachers fulfilling complementary roles of tutors. Children are also capable of self-learning through the internet.

For children with access to a PC, the "seamless" learning experiences of school and home encourages independent learning skills and the self-management of time. These are qualities that will be

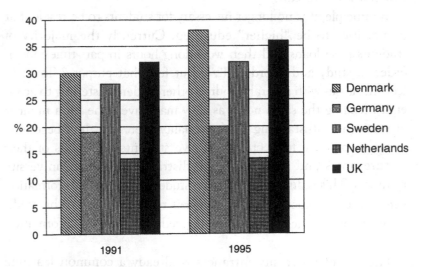

Proportion of new university entrants aged 25 or older 1991–95 (selected EU countries)
Source: Eurostat Social Portrait of Europe 1998

required by tomorrow's virtual organisations. On the other hand, a greater focus upon PC-based learning experiences could inhibit the development of inter-personal skills and the ability to co-operate with others in groups.

▶ Universities face new demands

The number of students attending universities is rising. The aim is for 50 per cent of all school leavers to go on to university by 2005 and the trend for the over 25s to study for degrees will also continue. University qualifications are recognised to improve employability, earnings and career development (even in "flattened" corporate structures). Moreover, the heightened occupational aspirations of women is another factor explaining the popularity of higher education. These trends, combined with the capabilities of ICTs, could lead to a dramatic re-structuring of higher education and the way in which it is delivered.

In principle, it is no longer necessary for students to be resident at universities to be "higher" educated. Currently the majority of students raise loans and then work long hours in part-time jobs in order to study and afford to live. But for what purpose? To sit in lecture classes with several hundred other students listening to academics reading the same notes as they may have done for a number of years (notwithstanding teacher quality exercises). It is becoming common practice for lecturers to give students hand-outs of their lecture notes and for these to be distributed through university intranets. This reduces the need for students to acquire information through face-to-face contact with their teachers. In fact, this traditional form of teaching is becoming redundant in an Information Age.

The use of university intranets is already a common learning methodology in the United States and Australia. Learning materials are distributed in this way and students prepare their projects working in "virtual teams". Students like this method of studying because they can learn flexibly and in a manner compatible with their other commitments. It is also much cheaper than traditional higher education methods.

One objection is that face-to-face interaction between students and teachers is vital for developing personal creativity. But, for the overwhelming majority of students, this simply does not happen under traditional teaching methods. A further argument is that learning through the internet would abolish the quality of student lifestyles. But these claims are more likely to be made by parents who attended universities in the 60s and 70s than students of today. Where is the quality of life working in supermarkets three hours each day to be in residence at a university?

The capabilities of information technologies in general, and the use of the internet in particular, offer opportunities for the learning process to be democratised and to be distributed to all sectors of

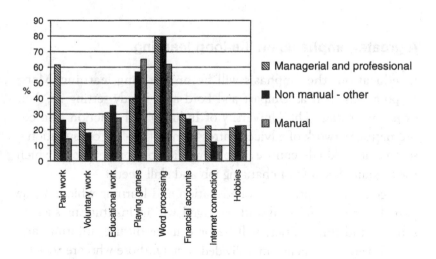

Use of PCs in the home by occupational group (%)
Source: ESRC British Household Panel Study 1998: University of Essex

society. It enables life-long learning. Universities of the future still have a vital role to play, although somewhat different to that of the past. Their research function will continue, but with a sharper applied focus. However, their teaching function could change dramatically because of ICTs. It will no longer be necessary for students to "go to university". Personal learning can be organised with a PC supplemented by short-term residential courses which emphasise "creative" interaction with fellow students and their teachers. The Open University offers a vision for the future.

The potential of the internet could mean that there are simply too many academics. For those who wish to hang on to a traditional academic lifestyle, the future looks bleak unless they are employed by the "high-branded" universities. Even so their roles are likely to change as they are compelled to embrace the potential of the new information technologies. They will no longer be able to rely upon last year's lecture notes. Instead, their students will expect value for money just as society will expect and, indeed, need a more creative labour force.

▶ A greater emphasis on life-long learning

In education, the emphasis will be on life-long learning. Many corporations such as Unipart and Ford are already setting up their own universities. The University of Industry will function as a co-ordinating network of advice centres – and of on-line consultation – so that individuals can develop portfolios of competencies which they require because of changing job and skill needs.

In general, the provision of education and learning which, in the past, has been packaged and managed within institutions such as schools and universities, will become more diffuse, informal and user-driven. This means in a divided society, those who are socially, economically and culturally "excluded" will benefit from this less than others. Domestic PCs and digital interactive TVs will be able to access information from all areas of the world, thereby enriching the cultural and educational experiences of Kim, Duncan and their child. For Maria and her family on the other hand, if there is a PC in the home it will be used for other, mainly entertainment purposes. The capabilities of ICTs will remain socially and culturally shaped.

▶ Some questions

▷ How can governments ameliorate the inequalities that limit the educational attainments of children in low-income households in the more impoverished regions of the country?

▷ How can private funding be attracted to the educational system to the advantage of those in greater need instead of reinforcing the privileges of "elite" schools and universities?

▷ How will universities re-structure, using ICTs so that degree qualifications are offered on a broader, more efficient and cost effective basis?

▷ What access to advice, and what mechanisms, will individuals need in developing their education and training portfolios for life-long learning?

▷ What should be the role of corporations in providing funds for learning at all levels of the education system system? Should it be through their own initiatives – as with setting up their own universities – or by providing funding through co-sponsorship of publicly funded schools and universities?

▷ What will be the future role of private school education in an information society? Will they be more effective at nurturing personal creativity or will they converge with their state managed counterparts?

▷ How far will universities become centres for short-term creative self-development, reducing the need for three-year, full-time degree programmes?

5

Lifestyles and leisure

- ▶ Will the market for home technologies grow?
- ▶ A future of long hours
- ▶ Becoming a 24 hour society
- ▶ Demographic changes create free time
- ▶ Interest grows in the self and self-development
- ▶ Staying young into middle age and beyond
- ▶ Room for individuality in the home
- ▶ Childhood grows shorter
- ▶ The internet fosters the global village
- ▶ Some questions

Lifestyles and leisure

▶ **Will the market for home technologies grow?**

According to some observers, the future will see the widespread use of domestic computer technology whereby vacuum cleaners operate automatically according to dust levels and robots undertake the boring chores. But any projections of the impact of ICTs in the home must take into account how time is used and the nature of gender roles. As more women occupy middle managerial and professional positions, a significant proportion will be living with partners in similar jobs. If long working hours continue as at the present, these couples will cope with household work in one of two ways. First, if a significant proportion of the population – younger men and particularly women – continue to earn low pay, then their employment as part-time cleaners, live-in nannies and housekeepers will increase. Second, if wage levels of home helpers increase making their employment expensive, Kim and Duncan will prefer to purchase labour-saving devices. This will lead to a market for innovative computer-based technological products for the home.

The growth in single professional persons and changing gender roles is also likely to be a force for innovation. When female partners enter into full time jobs, men take on more domestic responsibilities. In the mid 1970s, 20 per cent of unpaid home tasks were undertaken by men. By the early 1990s, this figure had increased to 35 per cent. With the more equal sharing of these duties between partners in full-time jobs there are likely to be growing pressures for domestic

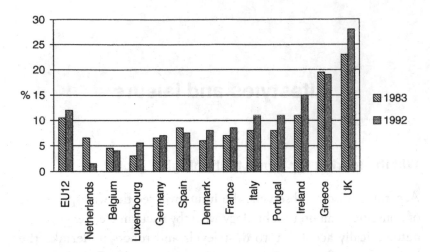

Weekly working hours in the EU – percentage of *men* working more than 48 hours 1983 and 1992
Source: Employment in Europe, EU Commission 1994

technological innovation and also demands for a reduction in working hours.

▶ A future of long hours

People in Britain work longer hours than in almost every other European country – only Portugal has a higher national average for men and women. Moreover, working hours are unlikely to fall over the next ten years. Claims that the future will be a leisure society are likely to prove false. Single managerial and professional employees are more committed to their jobs, see work as a "central life interest" and work longer hours. Long working hours will also be supported by the increasing numbers of self-employed who work longer hours than employees.

▶ Becoming a 24 hour society

Long working hours are likely to be unsociable with severe effects for family and leisure patterns and personal lifestyles. Compared with most other European countries, more men and women in Britain "sometimes" and "usually" work nights; the respective averages are 32 per cent and 8 per cent. They are also more likely to work on Saturdays and Sundays. This trend is set to continue as Britain becomes a 24 hour society. Retailing is a key driver in longer working hours as seven day shopping has knock-on effects for transportation and distribution, delivery systems, communications, catering and entertainment. Work patterns for Craig, Maria and her children are likely to feature long, irregular hours around which lifestyles and family patterns will have to be arranged. Work will become more rather than less significant.

▶ Demographic changes create free time

The amount of free time in society will increase because of the ageing of the population and the growing proportion of those over retirement age. Early retirement is likely to remain popular. And, even if early retirement schemes were to become less attractive and the financial costs of leaving the labour market more acute, a culture of early retirement is likely to persist. A lifestyle has now emerged among affluent groups in which, post-employment, personal freedom is attractive. It will be the lower income groups that will be disadvantaged as the need to work into old age will be a necessity. Kim, Rachel and Duncan can enjoy working careers before taking early retirement so that they can travel, relax and develop their various personal creative talents. For Craig and Maria, their futures are likely to be those of uncertainty, followed by a retirement with bouts of ill health and minor disabilities.

Growing numbers of time-rich and cash-rich older consumers will

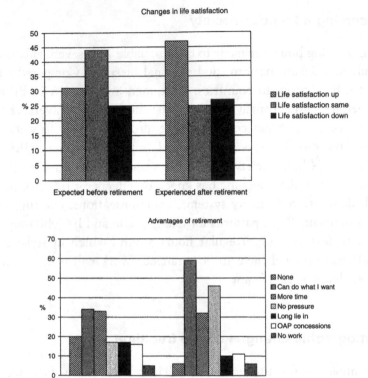

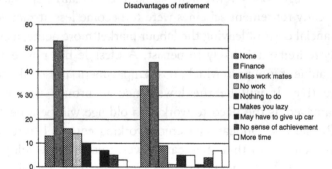

How the retired react to retirement

Source: Leisure Consultants (1998) "Transforming the future: rethinking free time and work"

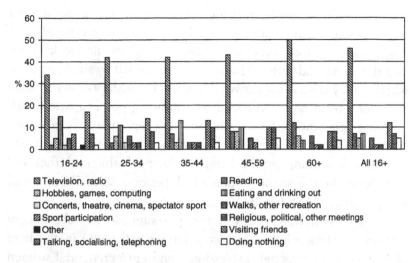

Free time use patterns of different age groups
Source. Social Trends, 1996 ONS

bring a re-orientation of corporate marketing, selling and retailing strategies. Not only will shopping patterns change but also the leisure, recreation, travel and entertainment industries.

There are already pointers in this direction. For example, the sea cruise industry continues to boom and, in order to attract advertising, different sectors of the media now focus more on the interests of older lifestyle groups.

▶ Interest grows in the self and self-development

With the ageing of the population and growing numbers enjoying higher education and life-long learning, personal creative pursuits will become attractive. There will be a greater focus upon self-development, through travel, cultural, intellectual and other activities. Outdoor pursuits such as walking, cycling and other "non-organised" interests will grow in popularity. This will lead to an expansion of interest groups that focus on the environment and national heritage.

The growth in single persons will reinforce the popularity of companionship groups and informal gatherings where people can meet. These will focus on those in their "young" middle age, between mid-thirties to mid-fifties. The focus upon the self by single persons, whether they are passing between couple relationships or living alone on a long term basis, will lead to a growing preoccupation with personal appearance, fitness and social acceptability. Demand for cosmetic surgery will rise. Personal concerns about self-identity will sustain a flourishing psychotherapy industry. Fashion, clothes and lifestyle will be the anchors upon which personal "brand" and social acceptability, will be based.

Living alone, however, will not pre-suppose the absence of emotional relationships. Personal relations will figure in the lives of live-alone managerial, professional and entrepreneurial women living in larger urban areas. For working class women in low paid jobs the picture will be different. While the former can engage in serial relations with little disruption to their personal material circumstances, this is not an option for working class women. Shifting from one partner to another will continue to involve financial hardships and, often, further personal and social obligations.

▶ Staying young into middle age and beyond

These trends, leading to a re-structuring of lifestyles, will bring a social re-definition of age. Not only will older people act and feel young but the lifestyles traditionally associated with different age categories will evaporate. Today, the London club scene is dominated by the preferences of professional, managerial and entrepreneurial "young" people in their thirties and forties and not, as in the past, by those in their late teens and early twenties. Adult-orientated rock and new Country and Western are music categories that appeal to the "young" forties and fifties. The music content of commercial radio stations and of Radio 2 reflect predominant music trends more

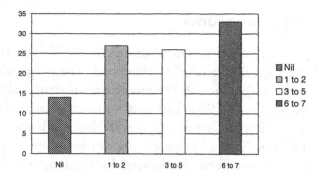

Number of shared main meals eaten in last week by children aged 11-15
Source ESRC; British Household Panel Study 1996, Youth questionnaire.

accurately than the more focused "minority" output of Radio 1. The themes of Hollywood movies, as well as of television drama, capture the lifestyles of those who in the past, according to traditional age categorisations, would be considered as "old" and therefore uninteresting. And yet the advertising and media industries have not yet woken up to these trends. They remain obsessed with the under-35s and stick to the now-redundant age and income marketing categories.

▶ Room for individuality in the home

For those in couple relationships and living with children, the home will be the focus for personal lifestyles. This trend will be even more pronounced as more and more people become self-employed or work from home. The household of the future will be "individualised", with each person – adults and children – sharing a common set of facilities but also able to pursue their own individual interests. This shift has been reinforced by the use of portable TVs and cheap hi-fi systems which convert children's bedrooms into personal leisure centres. The purchase of domestic PCs is a continuation of this trend.

▶ Childhood grows shorter

For couples with older children, shared family life will continue to erode through the "ageing" of childhood. The independence of teenagers (which began with the emergence of youth culture and popular music in the 1950s and 1960s) has now been gained by pre-teenagers. Divorce rates and the break-up of living together relationships has "forced" many children to be independent at an early age. This has been encouraged by teaching and learning techniques in schools. Also, the growth of a marketing segment that focuses exclusively upon the purchasing preferences of pre-teenage children. Their fashion preferences are now big business. Dedicated satellite television channels and weekly magazines for pre-teenagers are growing fast.

▶ The internet fosters the global village

The internet's use as a source of information, education and learning, and developing personal communities of interest will grow

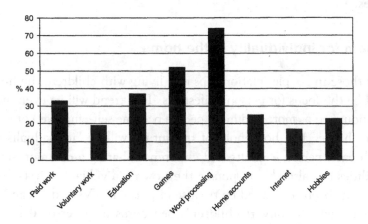

Domestic use of PCs in UK, 1997 (homes with computers = 29%)
Source: ESRC; British Household Panel Study 1998

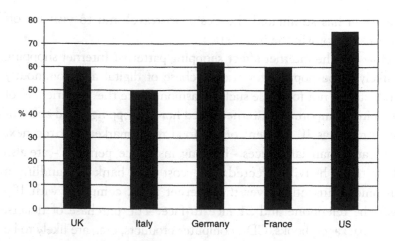

Projected growth of e-commerce – domestic PC penetration, 2004
Source: DTI Virtual Society Initiative

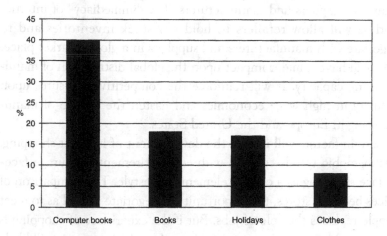

Percentage of different products presently purchased on the internet
Source: Financial Times, 1999

significantly. The use of email for maintaining personal contacts, as well as for developing friendships groups on a global basis, will be pronounced. This will stimulate more cosmopolitan interests. Just as television has stimulated the desire to travel and to visit far off places, so, too, will the internet.

How will the internet affect shopping patterns? Internet shopping is likely to be popular for the purchase of digital and commodity products but not for those such as fashion where the "experience" of shopping is important. Internet-based home shopping could account for as much as 10 per cent of the food retail market over the next few years. Financial services – banking, insurance, pensions – are also likely to be heavily affected. The cost to a bank of handling a customer transaction over the internet is 1p, compared with 10p over the telephone and £1 face-to-face. The purchase of tickets, travel packages, books, CDs, computer products, etc., are likely to be handled electronically.

The internet is likely to become significant "upstream" in e-business rather than e-commerce. That is, transactions between retailers, suppliers and manufacturers. The "immediacy" of internet trading will allow retailers to hold low stock inventories and to negotiate with manufacturers and suppliers in a global market place. This will have a major impact upon the global distribution of manufacturing capacity. It will reinforce the competitive pressures upon industry in high wage economies and hasten the demise of manufacturing in Europe and the United States.

Certain factors will inhibit the development of internet shopping. Demographic trends coupled with early retirement encourage face-to-face shopping as a central element of lifestyle. The comparison of prices between stores, the opportunity to negotiate as well as to meet people replaces the role of jobs. But if the experience of shopping is important in the purchase of a product, then the internet is still likely to be used as a marketing tool for consumers to gather information and view products. This is likely to be the role of the internet in the purchase and sale of houses. For various products and services, consumers will be able to search a global marketplace. But fears about the security of financial transactions and high brand loyalty will prevent this from becoming more than a market niche. "Anoraks" may search the internet for the cheapest computer software but global shopping is unlikely to be of major significance unless consumers become less loyal in their spending patterns than they have been in the past. Internet shopping will also be difficult for the "information poor" who lack the technical skills to use the technology. They are also high credit risk and restricted in their electronic purchases.

When home shopping is used it is likely to be through interactive television rather than PCs. The present partnership between BT and BSkyB suggests the direction, the assumption being that for the mass consumer market, television is more user friendly and less alienating than computer technology. The provision of interactive digital television will probably play a greater role in making Britain an information society than computer-based delivery systems. The two will converge but the requirements of Craig and Maria compared with those of Rachel, Kim and Duncan will remain different.

▶ Some questions

▷ If traditional market research categories based upon socio-economic and age categories are becoming redundant, what criteria should determine relevant "lifestyle" market groupings?

▷ How will the advertising and media industries need to re-structure to meet the needs of "1001" life style tribes?

▷ How far can post offices and shops in rural areas be "re-invented" as e-commerce ordering, distribution and technical support centres for socially excluded rural populations?

▷ In what consumer markets is internet shopping likely to have its major impact? How is this likely to affect the responses of traditional supermarket retailers?

▷ What are some of the challenges for retailers when shopping increasingly becomes regarded as a lifestyle, leisure activity?

▷ Until there is a convergence between television and computing technologies, which of these two pathways are likely to be the more significant for developing home shopping?

6

Cities and communities

- ▶ The impact of social change on communities
- ▶ Marked regional inequalities remain
- ▶ Single persons rejuvenate the inner cities
  - Demographics will change communities
  - Locality continues to shape lifestyles
  - The impact of industrial clusters on local culture
- ▶ The psychological importance of Community
- ▶ The changing role of local government
- ▶ How local government can respond to new demands
- ▶ Elected mayors may stimulate public interest
- ▶ Some questions

Cities and communities

▶ **The impact of social change on communities**

The reality of macro social change is experienced in people's everyday lives in the context of their personal relations, neighbourhoods and communities. Traditionally, the lifestyles of communities were shaped by their industrial characteristics. The continuing shift in the economy from a manufacturing to an information base will have a major impact on the composition and structure of Britain's cities and communities.

Economic re-structuring will continue to shape the fabric of cities, towns and communities in Britain. The globalisation of supply chains and shift in manufacturing capacity to South East Asia is reinforcing the economic decline of some communities and regions while in others, the growth of information-based industries is leading to rapid economic development. The outcome is a diversity of communities with the local-based lifestyles of Craig, Maria and her children being different to those enjoyed by Rachel, Duncan and Kim. While those of the former are dictated by economic compulsion and constraint, those of the latter are characterised by diversity and choice. The outcome is a society consisting of those who on the one hand, are socially, culturally and economically excluded and others who are economically and sociologically incorporated.

Economic change has brought about the destruction of traditional household, neighbourhood and community relations. In the past, the old industrial towns consisted of social networks which functioned as

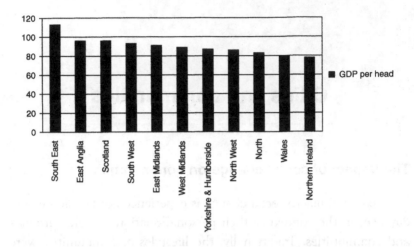

GDP per head in UK Regions compared with EU average
Source: Review of the Economy and Employment 1998/1999, Institute for Employment Research, University of Warwick

modes of social integration and informal social control. These, with their routines, duties and obligations offered life-style certainty and security. They gave individuals identity and status, derived from their roles as neighbours, friends, family members and local residents. This is not to romanticise. There were conflicts, tensions, prejudices and jealousies. These environments often restricted achievement and creativity. Sometimes they nurtured racism and certainly sexism.

▶ Marked regional inequalities remain

Differences in the living standards of the various communities and regions of Britain are likely to persist. While Regional Development Agencies, the job creation initiatives of local authorities and policies of national government may ameliorate some of these, the restructuring of global supply chains, the shift of manufacturing to other countries and the development of Britain as an information

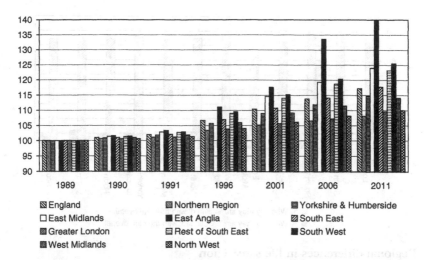

☒ England   ▨ Northern Region   ▤ Yorkshire & Humberside
☐ East Midlands   ■ East Anglia   ▨ South East
▨ Greater London   ▨ Rest of South East   ■ South West
▦ West Midlands   ▨ North West

1989 Based projections of increase in numbers of households by region (1989 = 100)

Source: Department of the Environment; Household Projections England 1989–2011: HMSO

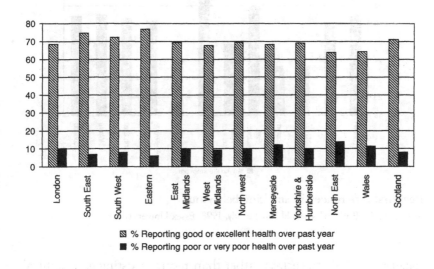

▨ % Reporting good or excellent health over past year
■ % Reporting poor or very poor health over past year

Regional differences in self reported health status over previous year

Source: ESRC British Household Panel Study 1998 University of Essex

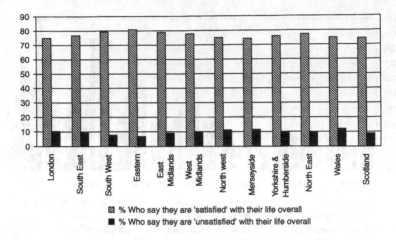

% Who say they are 'satisfied' with their life overall

% Who say they are 'unsatisfied' with their life overall

Regional differences in life satisfaction
Source: ESRC British Household Panel Study, 1998, Essex University

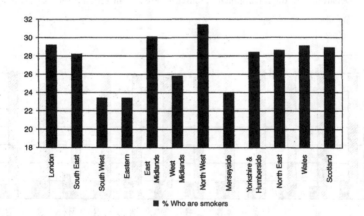

% Who are smokers

Regional differences in smoking behaviour
Source: ESRC British Household Panel Study, 1998, Essex University

society are likely to sustain rather than reduce existing geographical inequalities.

From matters of health to those of wealth, regional contrasts exist

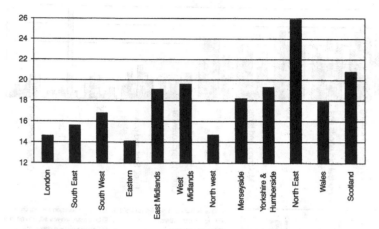

% **Visiting their GP more than 5 times in last year by region**
Source: ESRC British Household Panel Study, 1998, Essex University

which are unlikely to disappear over the next decade. The outcome of these inequalities is likely to be the continuing migration of population from Scotland and the north of England to the southern parts of the country. These contrasts have important ramifications for the provision of state services, the national health service and local government. The "socially excluded" will place greater demands upon publicly-funded services and, in those areas in which poverty is concentrated, the more privileged – such as Rachel, Kim and Duncan – will "opt out" for what they perceive to be better services through private insurance. They will see themselves as "customers" and therefore, purchasers of services in ways in which Craig, Maria and her children are excluded.

▶ Single persons rejuvenate the inner cities

If regional inequalities continue, so too will diversities within and between large urban communities. Large urban areas continue to be segregated on the basis of income, occupation and lifestyle. Greater

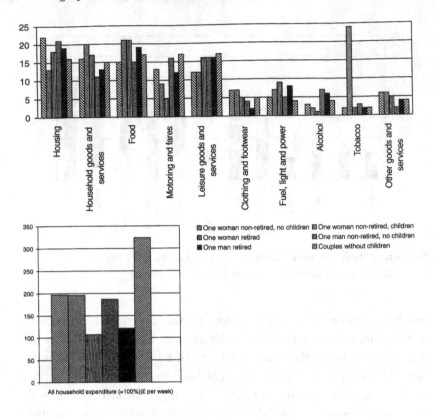

Household expenditure by type of household 1996–1997
ONS Family Expenditure Survey 1997

diversity has now become evident with the growth of new cultures associated with ethnic communities. These have introduced variety in lifestyles, patterns of spending and consumption which are now key ingredients of modern urban mosaics.

The growth of single person households among the young and the "middle aged" is likely to be near the centres of major cities. Housing projects geared to this market sector will focus upon their leisure, health and personal security needs. Those with more traditional family or household patterns will live in the outer suburbs where the provision of quality schooling, education and childcare will be concentrated. The lifestyle of Rachel and her friends will shape the predominant cultures of urban neighbourhoods – just as they do today in Islington, Wandsworth and other parts of London. These are the localities within which fast food outlets, delicatessens, wine bars, clubs and 24-hour stores will be concentrated. Cosmopolitan and fashionable lifestyles will be focused in these areas. As today, it is in these urban areas – not only in London but also in a more restricted sense in Edinburgh, Glasgow, Cardiff and some of the larger provincial cities – that experimentation and innovation in lifestyles will be most pronounced. The residents will be the targeted marketing categories of the advertising industry and large sectors of the media. They will continue to be the high spenders on travel, consumer products and services. For women, that is, until the first child arrives.

Demographics will change communities

Other communities of interest, located in particular geographical areas, will also account for diversities in the provision of amenities and services. Trends for the retired to live in the South West are unlikely to change. The more privileged are likely to segregate themselves in "secure" housing developments in Britain, Spain, Portugal and Florida. For increasing numbers – because of early retirement, extended life expectancy and the economics of house building – theirs will be a lifestyle of security guards (at the entrance to estates) and video cameras. Following early retirement, there will be a preoccupation with personal health, appearance and social acceptability. Shopping and socialising will be the axis of their lifestyles with personal hobbies and special interests taking over the role, for most, of their previous jobs.

Locality continues to shape lifestyles

How significant will "locality" be in the future? Will the internet and ICTs reduce its importance as a shaper of lifestyles? While the internet offers the capability for people to interact and maintain contact with a broader geographical network of friends and acquaintances, it will not negate the importance of neighbourhood. As a result, the make-up of communities will continue to be diverse, reflecting socio-economic, demographic and lifestyle factors. These will shape the facilities that are available and the appeal that communities will have for different social groupings. If, in the past, the importance of locality was driven by the availability of local employment this will now be replaced by the attractions of good shopping facilities, quality education, "law and order" and the "brand reputation" of the community.

The impact of industrial clusters on local culture

Locality is also important for its "clustering" effects. In the industrial era, manufacturing companies tended to be concentrated where there was the availability of resources – technical, geological and human. In Britain today there is the clustering of high technology companies in the Thames Valley, parts of Scotland and in the Cambridge area. Equally, the attraction of Bristol and Reading for financial services and the centre of London, despite high costs, for the public relations and advertising industries.

These geographical clusters generate their own cultures which shape local infrastructures. Educational institutions are compelled to respond to their employment requirements, local authorities to the quality of life expectations of employees and other agencies to communication and transport demands. Local cultures are also affected as employees share similarities in occupational, leisure and lifestyle interests which again are reflected in the provision of amenities provided by both public and private sectors. Information technology clusters are emerging which give the Thames Valley greater affinity with San Francisco than with Sunderland. In this way, "information" regions are being plucked from their national hinterlands to be incorporated within globally-integrated industries.

► The psychological importance of community

In an Information Age, the notion of community also takes on a psychological dimension. Community becomes a source of personal attachment and psychological identification for those in jobs that require them to be geographically mobile. In an uncertain world where jobs are insecure and futures are unpredictable, living in a risk society reinforces the importance of community in a symbolic sense. Individuals obtain a sense of "place", of attachment to the communities in which they live. If they are professional men and women such as Rachel or Kim and Duncan, they may make little use of local amenities. The role of the local authority may be of no relevance to them in terms of the quality of health, education and welfare services provided. Equally, they may make little use of local shopping or leisure facilities. But in a symbolic or psychological sense, "place" of belonging is home and in this sense, "community" is important. In this way, the status or "brand" of community is a relevant factor.

The role of the local media can also be significant. A key function of local radio and the press is to nurture a sense of community identification. In those localities where the community is not a source of employment, the local media can create the sense of community. It shapes its image, its brand and with symbols that individuals feel they can identify. Football clubs fulfil a similar role. They fill the gap created by the anomie of 1960s urban regeneration, 1980s industrial decline and the break up of conventional family patterns.

▶ The changing role of local government

Geographical localities are important in relation to other factors such as education, shopping, transport and law and order. Personal accessibility is a major determinant of lifestyle and accounts for its growing political significance. It also impacts upon the quality of communities and the environment. The growth in expectations for improved transport and environment is likely to lead to a shift towards a greater provision of mass transport services through rapid transit systems such as light railways, monorails and electrically-operated buses.

A common demand for good local government focuses upon law and order. With an increase in single person households, the ageing of the population and the declining number of young people, it is likely that the rate of crime will fall over the next decade. But in a "risk" society, the fear of crime will increase. This will put growing pressures on the police to extend their intelligence gathering activities and make greater use of ICTs to maintain law and order. Improved technology will enable the police to engage in immediate response policies and to extend their surveillance over public life. By using ICTs, the police will be able to change public expectations about police "visibility" and reduce their dependency upon personal presence at minor crimes. Possibly a bigger challenge will be for the police to heighten their level of trust among citizens. With new forms of security architecture in a "law-and-order" society, the visible role of the police could be reduced.

▶ How local government can respond to new demands

New demands from communities will have implications for local government. The use of ICTs will encourage the adoption of new employment and work practices. Working from home can also generate a greater concern about community amenities. Some local

Legend:
□ Great deal
■ Fair amount
■ Just a little
■ Hardly anything
■ Don't know

How much do you know about your local council?
Source: MORI Local Government Presentation February 1999

authorities are already ahead of many private sector organisations in adopting new management philosophies. They have embarked upon strategic outsourcing and sub-contract out many of their activities. Many have adopted "family friendly" employment policies encouraging part-time and flexi-work, as well as job sharing. Some already operate as network organisations, with a small core of purchasers negotiating quality control with external providers. They are also encouraging home-working, allowing employees to operate in virtual teams.

Pressures for cost reduction and value for money are likely to compel local authorities to develop these strategies further. They will take on the characteristics of facilities management companies, defining their role as the "overseers" of rural and urban infrastructures which are provided and managed by private companies. This change will be possible because citizens are becoming less interested in local political processes. Only a minority of people are aware of the names of their councillors and few show any inclination to become involved in local politics.

Most citizens see themselves as consumers of services rather than responsible for deciding the means by which they are provided. If this attitude changes little in the future, attempts to encourage greater citizen involvement in local government affairs through the use of internet technologies are likely to little impact. Popular involvement is only evident over particular issues, such as the proposed closure of a hospital or school.

▶ Elected mayors may stimulate public interest

The election of mayors is likely to have some impact on popular interest in local politics. Election campaigns between competing individuals are likely to "personalise" issues such as local transport systems and law and order. This will create a greater transparency in local decision-making and could heighten citizen interest. But, as with politics today, it is likely to be Kim and Duncan who will set the agendas for debate rather than Craig and Maria. For the growing, although minority, proportion of the population enjoying the urban and cosmopolitan lifestyle of Rachel and her friends, local politics will be of little interest. Even when Jane decides to have a child, her private purchase of hospital treatment, pre-school care and then of education services will lead her to take a highly detached, managerial interest. That is, unless a specific issue impacts directly upon her personal life such as a road widening or office development scheme. Then, she and her friends will be among the first to mobilise to protect their self-interests. Otherwise, local government is unlikely to be more than the domain of a public-spirited middle class who claim to be acting in the interests of the "community". In other words, fighting for such issues as environment, law and order and improved local transport.

▶ Some questions

▷ Should local government remain responsible for providing education and welfare services if national government is committed to reducing regional patterns of social and economic exclusion?

▷ In what areas of local government can there be a wider adoption of ICTs with subsequent cost reduction and improved service delivery?

▷ How can interest in local government be re-established and citizen interest and engagement re-kindled?

▷ To what extent could facilities management companies take over many local government functions with significant improvements in quality of service delivery and substantial cost reductions?

▷ How far will city mayors generate greater public interest in local politics?

▷ In what ways will the growth of "information cities", reinforce regional polarisation and national fragmentation? How far can governments ameliorate these trends?

▷ How far can the police utilise ICTs for improving law and order without excessively intruding upon personal privacy?

▷ Who will cater for the housing, social and welfare of the low paid and the excluded in affluent information, high technology regional clusters?

▷ To what extent do knowledge pools and resource sharing offered by the capabilities of ICTs render redundant the independence of local authorities with their subsequent high cost structures?

7

Politics, government and the state

- ▶ The end of political ideology
- ▶ A cynical electorate
- ▶ Quality of life and "me" politics
- ▶ The limitations of governments in a global economy
- ▶ Demographics bring greater demands on the state
- ▶ The potential of ICTs to revolutionise government
- ▶ Civil service cultures as barriers to change?
- ▶ ICTs: opportunities or threats?
- ▶ Virtual government needs an educated society
- ▶ Some questions

Politics, government and the state

▶ The end of political ideology

The nature of politics has changed fundamentally over past decades. The "end of ideology" has been much discussed. The traditional values that separated the Conservative and Labour parties are no longer relevant. The old-style differentiation between "left" and "right" mean little to new generations of voters. What is more important to them are issues. Political debate focuses upon issues that are personalised and immediate to voters. Despite declining allegiances to political parties, there is likely to be continuing loyalty in voting patterns among different socio-economic categories.

What is changing is how political parties are perceived by the electorate. At the end of the 20th century, neither the Labour nor the Conservative party has a clearly-defined electoral identity compared with the early 1980s. Then, Thatcherism stamped the Conservatives with the free market, the cold war and privatisation. Michael Foot, the then leader of the Labour Party, associated them with unilateral nuclear disarmament, nationalisation and general state intervention in economic life. Today, both parties are vaguely associated with issues rather than with such ideologies. This is likely to sustain a high proportion of "floating voters" who have no firm political allegiance.

These current trends reinforce the ability of governing parties to remain in office and adds to the difficulties of those in opposition to demonstrate electoral credibility. Each of the major parties, in a post ideology era, can steal each other's clothes while, at the same time, focusing upon the issues that are of immediate and practical relevance to electors. What are these likely to be over the next ten years?

▶ A cynical electorate

For Maria and Craig it is difficult to see any significant change in their cynicism towards politics. In 2010, just as today, they will regard politicians as corrupt and self-interested. As with their predecessors in the 1990s, their attitudes will be contradictory in that they want low taxes but high welfare and social benefits and an effective state-funded health service. They will regard no political party as representing their interests but if they do bother to vote, they will vote Labour. Essentially, however, they have little interest in either politics or political issues.

The political alienation of the socially and economically excluded means that the agenda for political debate will be determined by the self-interests of Rachel, Duncan and Kim. They may be concerned about continuing poverty and the debts of third world countries but they view these as inevitable.

▶ Quality of life and "me" politics

In the first decade of the 21st century, the same issues will continue to be at the heart of political debate as in the 1990s; that is, education, the welfare state and health services. In addition to these, the environment, transport and the production and consumption of food products are likely to assume greater significance.

Quality of life will be a key political issue. Its importance results from factors such as an increase in the number of university graduates, the growth of high skill, expert and creative jobs associated with the emerging information society and the increase in middle-age single person households. The consequence will be political demands

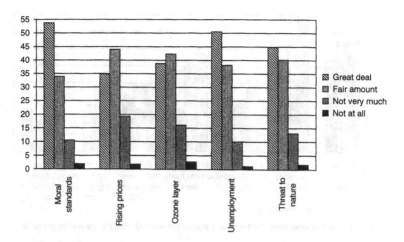

Key political issues 1990s – extent to which adults think that each issue is "a cause for concern" (row percentages)
Source: ESRC British Household Panel Study, Essex University 1997

for tighter regulation over the production, manufacture and distribution of foodstuffs. Supermarkets will face growing pressure to sell authenticated natural products and governments will be held responsible for monitoring the food chain more closely. Personal health and fitness will become a political issue and this is likely to lead to greater regulation in relation to urban congestion, pollution and the environment.

A key element on the political agenda for improving the quality of life is likely to be the nature of work and its impact upon personal health and lifestyles. Legislation will probably be needed to force companies to introduce family-friendly policies in terms of flexible, part-time and job-share working hours. The capabilities of ICTs already allow a significant proportion of work tasks to be undertaken at home. But in many companies the management culture continues to associate corporate commitment with long working hours on site. Legislation will probably be required to change this culture, particularly when it is recognised that prolonged and extensive working

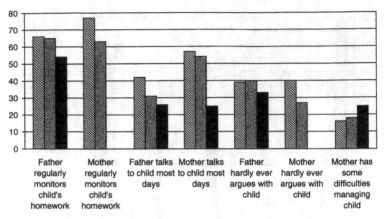

Father regularly monitors child's homework | Mother regularly monitors child's homework | Father talks to child most days | Mother talks to child most days | Father hardly ever argues with child | Mother hardly ever argues with child | Mother has some difficulties managing child

▨ 30-40 hours worked/week ▩ 41-48 hours worked per week ■ 49-60 hours worked per week

Family communication by parents' working hours (percentages)
Source: ESRC British Household Panel Study, University of Essex, 1998

hours can have negative, and sometimes permanently detrimental, effects upon personal health and relationships.

In terms of personal values it is likely that "employment" will be redefined and incorporated within personal concerns about health, psychological well-being and the general quality of life. This process will be reinforced by increasing job insecurity, career instabilities and a growing recognition of the potential personal costs of allowing "work" to be the central life interest.

▶ The limitations of governments in a global economy

The rise of the global economy will make it even more difficult for governments to respond to these changing political demands. The growth of information industries that operate in the global economy limit the power of governments in various ways. Information-based corporations, whether they are pharmaceutical, software, biotechno-logical or financial services, have greater geographical mobility than manufacturing industries. They, and their employees, can easily shift their sites of operation between countries depending upon the conditions offered them by national governments. The capabilities of information and communication technologies allow companies to be managed globally and to be located according to local legal, employment and fiscal regimes.

A further constraint on the ability of governments to enforce legislation to improve the quality of working and personal life is the continuing growth of small and medium sized enterprises. With an increasing proportion of the labour force either self-employed, or owning or working in small firms, it will be difficult to implement legislation intended to regulate the length of working hours, flexi-time and other work practices.

▶ Demographics bring greater demands on the state

A culture of personal independence will compel governments to embrace low tax regimes. Yet the demands on government spending

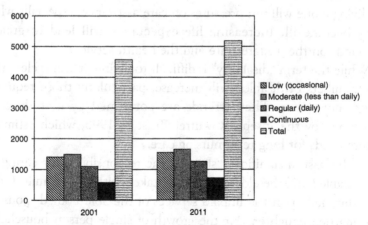

Care needed for numbers of disabled adults aged 60 and over (thousands)
Source: Institute and Faculty of Actuaries (1993), Financing Long Term Care in Great Britain

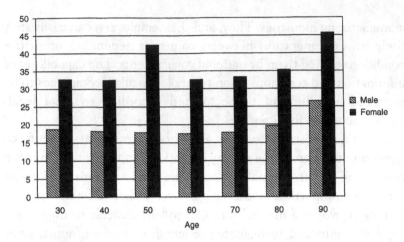

Likelihood of needing long term nursing care at some time in the future (rate per 100)
Source: Joseph Rowntree Foundation, 1996

are likely to be greater in the future because of demographic drivers such as the growth of single person households and the ageing of the population. The increase in the percentage of men over the age of 60 living alone will put pressures on care assistance, especially when they become ill. Increasing life expectancy will lead to greater demands on the welfare state and the health service.

While the term "disability" is difficult to define, it seems clear that the numbers of disabled will increase, particularly those requiring continuous care. These trends are confirmed by a study commissioned by the Joseph Rowntree Trust in 1996, which estimates future needs for long term nursing care.

In the past, a significant share of the responsibility for caring for the disabled and the elderly was undertaken within the family. Often this duty fell upon the unpaid services of the able-bodied spouse or the married daughter. But the growth of single person households, the increasing proportion of women engaged in full-time as well as part-time jobs, and the growing complexity of personal relationships through "split-ups" and divorce, makes care within the family even less of an option than at present.

Care for the very elderly will continue to be institutionalised. For those with minor disabilities, information and communication technologies will allow people to monitor their health at home and to enjoy independent lifestyles. Care costs can be reduced by new technologies. Even so, demands upon government expenditure are likely to increase so that health, education and welfare provision will become more selective. Means testing is likely to become more pronounced with those who can afford it, buying their own pension, health treatment and long-term care. Government finances could be improved by the widespread application of information and communication technologies that would enable more effective administration at a lower cost. But will civil service cultures allow the capabilities of ICTs to be exploited fully?

▶ The potential of ICTs to revolutionise government

New technologies have the capacity to revolutionise many government services by delivering considerable cost savings. The present government declared in 1998 an objective of one quarter of all state procurements being made via e-commerce by 2004. This will allow many government departments to rationalise their administrative processes. Equally, if the potential for homeworking by civil servants was implemented, the need for high overheads associated with location in prime London sites could be reduced – to say nothing about the reduction in traffic congestion.

The challenges facing government over the next ten years are likely to concern not only cost reduction but also improved service provision. Citizens will have high expectations of government service standards which they will expect to match those offered by the best performing supermarkets. It means that over the next decade the

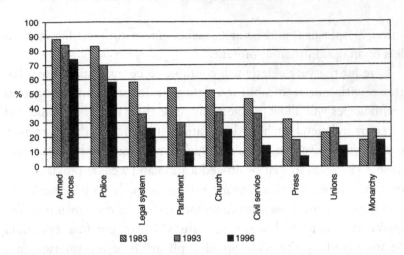

Percentages reporting a lot or a great deal of faith in different institutions
Source: Henley Centre: Planning for Social Change 1996/97

civil service will need to regain its "brand integrity", by re-establishing the trust that the public has in its institutions.

ICTs will play a key role in ensuring the government delivers its services more effectively. In future citizens are likely to demand an immediate and personalised response to their requirements, whether this is the Health Service, Inland Revenue, the Benefits Agency or the DTI. Citizens are unlikely, however, to expect face-to-face negotiations with government officials except under exceptional circumstances. This means that in terms of both its internal operating procedures and its external relations, government departments could, over the next ten years, lead the way in becoming "virtual" organisations. By embracing the capabilities of information and communication technologies, they could co-ordinate both internal departmental and inter-departmental processes for meeting citizen needs and thereby provide more efficient and cost effective services.

The shift towards virtual government could be reinforced by the continuing out-sourcing of many "in-house" functions through strat-

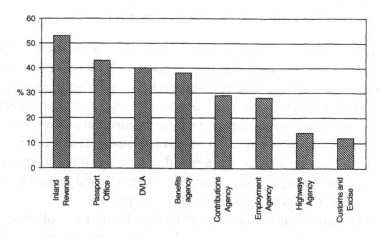

Percentage of adults who have phoned agency hotline in past year
Source: Henley Centre: Teleculture – The Citizen Speaks

egic partnerships and other collaborative mechanisms with private sector service providers. This is likely to occur in areas of health and education as well as in construction projects and transportation systems. Already there are such initiatives in primary and secondary education. It would be surprising if pharmaceutical and insurance companies do not become more involved in areas of presently state-funded primary health care. As a result of such initiatives, the civil service would greatly reduce its number of directly employed staff. Instead it would function as an enabling authority, operating as a purchaser of services which are delivered to citizens in collaboration with different private sector providers. Of course, a strategic core would remain but not in its present-day 19th century administrative form. An information society will require an Information Age governmental process. The current dependency upon paper will be superseded by intranet and internet technologies. Equally, present departmental structures reflect bygone work patterns and citizen life styles. New configurations are required to respond more effectively to changing citizen demands.

▶ Civil service cultures as barriers to change?

Whether these capabilities – with their cost savings and citizen benefits – can be fully realised depends on how far civil service culture can change. The civil service is currently structured upon clearly defined protocols and procedures. These are not only paper-based but determine all aspects of the governmental process, ranging from job descriptions to authority relations and personal careers. To challenge and to change these would require the transformation of total organisational processes as well as the required human capital to manage the technology-based operating processes.

Another potential obstacle to change is the issue of personal security and the extent to which ICTs can safeguard citizen confidentiality. If government services are structured on the basis of co-ordinated and shared data on citizens, there is the legitimate fear that information will be misused and that individual freedoms could be curtailed.

▶ ICTs: opportunities or threats?

The challenges facing government in its implementation of information and communication technologies reflect many of the issues surrounding their continuing adoption in all spheres of life. ICTs offer unforeseen opportunities and, within these, inherent threats. The former include the greater accessibility to appropriate information upon which choices and decisions can be made while the threats concern personal confidentiality and intrusions upon privacy. As far as government institutions are concerned, the widespread adoption of internet technologies has the potential to make decision-making processes not only quicker but also more transparent. It means that broader networks of interest groups can be consulted within shorter time frames. In this way, legislative processes can be quickened and democratic processes reinforced. On the other hand, the shift to virtual, spontaneous government could reinforce existing patterns of exclusion. The adoption of internet technologies may motivate Kim and Duncan to express their opinions about a road widening scheme, but they are unlikely to be utilised by Maria and Craig. Such persisting social and economic inequalities present the major barrier to virtual government.

▶ Virtual government needs an educated society

In theory companies can transfer their entire operations to e-commerce. They can identify particular niches in the market and focus their strategies upon these. This is not possible for government. The delivery of services has to be both universal and equal. While a large proportion of the population is not computer literate, citizen services cannot be provided solely in electronic form. This inhibits government departments from becoming ICT-based, prevents them from drastically revolutionising their administrative processes and obtaining large cost savings.

In future, government departments such as the Inland Revenue are likely to differentiate the delivery of their services according to different citizen niches. But it is only when all citizens are connected to the internet that forms of virtual government can be fully implemented. The timeframe for this is likely to extend beyond 2010 and long after it is normal for every school child to have access to a computer. Until that time the role of government will be shaped as much by the pressures and demands stemming from Britain's unequal social structure as from the capabilities of information and communication technologies. The different citizen expectations of Rachel, Kim, Duncan, Maria and Craig will be as equally influential as the latest technological wizardry of Bill Gates.

▶ Some questions

▷ Post-ideology politics is likely to continue. The charisma of politicians and the "presentation" of policies will constitute the substance of political debate. How will this affect party loyalties and affiliations?

▷ How will structural changes in the economy, particularly the growth of small and medium size enterprises and the expansion of self-employment, affect the capabilities for government employment legislation to be effectively implemented?

▷ What are the likely effects of the increase in life expectancy and associated rates of disability for governments funding of the health services and the welfare state?

▷ How far can information and communication technologies be utilised to reduce the costs of government administration? In what ways do these allow administrative processes to be reconfigured to meet the very different needs of citizens in an information, but unequal, society?

▷ How can personal privacy be protected in a society when government makes greater use of information and communication technologies?

▷ To what extent will continuing social and economic exclusion among sectors of citizens inhibit the widespread adoption of information and communication technologies in government service provision?

▷ How can the capabilities of information and communication technologies be fully utilised to open up government consultative processes and quicken legislative programmes?

8

Towards the future

Towards the future

▶ Britain without vision or identity

Britain lacks an integrated and coherent national, as distinct from state identity. As a national state, it incorporates the identities of four nations: England, Wales, Scotland and Northern Ireland. Each of these has aspirations, values and cultures that, until recently, were excluded from the arena of political debate (with the exception of Northern Ireland). This limits the value of discussion of what kind of country Britain wants or should be in the future. Possibly, it has no future as an integrated, unitary state. The separate nations of present-day Britain will evolve their own semi-autonomous political and cultural focus within a more integrated European political economy. Each of these will develop their own particular future visions, out of which the disparity of the four separate nations, so long concealed under English political hegemony, will become more apparent.

▶ The impact of demographics

Putting these complexities aside, it is clear that a key driver for change in the future will be changing demographics as well as the continuing impact of technological change and the increasing integration of the global economy. The ageing of the population will have major consequences for most aspects of society, ranging from the role of the health service and the welfare state, to patterns of retailing. The changing composition of households – fewer children, more single persons, high rates of divorce and the "churning" of partners – will have repercussions for lifestyles, patterns of spending and housing markets.

▶ A demanding population

The decline of manual employment and the growth of managerial, professional, technical and creative jobs will have implications for the educational system, as well as for patterns of personal spending, lifestyles and even political debate. As the population becomes more knowledgeable, traditionalism, deference and acquiescence break down. People become more demanding of the services they receive not only from retail organisations but also publicly-provided services ranging from health and education to policing and the environment. Such a population is also more cynical, distrusting and suspicious. The focus is upon the self, the immediate and the spontaneous. Much of this is driven by the anxieties and uncertainties generated by changing personal relations, technological change and the re-structuring of the global economy.

The globalisation of the economy

The continuing impact of globalisation affects not only the nature of the economy but also people's lives through their employment opportunities and working conditions. As companies compete in global markets, the knock-on effects for corporate efficiency through cost reductions and the need for continuous product innovation, affects people's training needs and job opportunities. Working lives become more uncertain and less predictable in both the short and longer term. Early retirement becomes a major attraction and part-time employment the norm for many. At the same time, employees renegotiate the "psychological contracts" they have with their employing organisations. Employees' attitude to work become short-term, instrumental and cynical – an orientation which spills over into a broader set of "lifestyle" attitudes that emphasise immediacy and living for the present. It also reinforces cynical, suspicious low-trust work cultures. This is one of the major barriers to Britain becoming a high-performing, innovative and creative economy.

Management as a barrier to national creativity

To compete in global markets, companies must embrace continuous innovation. This can only be achieved by leveraging intellectual capital and the creativity of employees. Before this can happen there must be high-trust cultures in both the corporate environment and the broader society. At present, too many businesses are structured and managed on the basis of low trust.

Management too often still demands employee compliance rather than encouraging personal creativity. Many employees feel disempowered and alienated, even in the "new" sectors of high technology. They do not feel themselves as stake-holders in the future of their companies and therefore lack incentive to be creative and innovative. To be competitive in the future global economy will require a revolution in the culture and practices of British management. Their attitudes and assumptions are the major barrier to Britain becoming a high performing creative economy. These also prevent organisations from realising the potential of ICTs for cutting costs through transforming work patterns. Far more companies need to take lessons from the "alternative" cultures and work patterns of Silicon Valley and the .com businesses.

Social exclusion as a barrier to creativity

Despite the culture of present-day political debate, Britain remains a divided society. Exclusion exists in many areas of economic, political and social life. This fosters resentment, antagonism, suspicion and low trust. Consumerism and mass culture conceals many of the more explicit forms of social exclusion in society. Even so, inequalities in opportunities and reward remain. In some aspects of life these have increased, as in the United States, over the past decade. Whether in terms of health and illness, life expectancy, attendance at the elite universities, employment conditions, income rewards or wealth ownership, Britain continues to be characterised by high rates of exclusion. With what outcomes? The ramifications for Britain's economy are significant. Individuals are orientated to "take out" of society as much as they can for the expenditure of as little effort as possible. The result is a short-term instrumentalism that pervades all spheres of social and economic life. This, in turn, generates feelings of alienation, lack of employee creativity and corporate innovation as well as various forms of deviant behaviour, including organised crime and drug dealing. Only in the entertainment industry do the experiences of exclusion have positive outcomes for leveraging individual and organisational creativity. The film industry offers some examples but more so does popular music. Different genres nurtured within "excluded" socio-economic environments have been a major force for innovation and change.

▶ The social context of ICTs

It is clear that any understanding of the impact of ICTs on society has to be interpreted within a broader social, economic and business context. This is a more realistic approach than that adopted by those who may be described as "utopian technologists". Although ICTs possess the capabilities for changing work and employment patterns, it is organisational cultures and practices that will determine whether such capabilities are realised. While, for example, employee "commitment" is measured by the hours spent in the office, the potential for increasing home-working, and reducing commuting and environmental pollution, will not be realised.

Although ICTs may support a huge growth in electronic shopping, this is unlikely to take off while retail shopping is central to personal lifestyles. For those who retire early, shopping will remain a central sphere for personal decision making, the exercise of personal judge- ment, as well as for social interaction. In other words, shopping replaces work as a "pivotal" interest. Conversely, there are single professional people who lack "free" time and who will grasp at the opportunity to shop through the internet. In other words, the impact of electronic commerce for some products and services will be greater than in others because of a range of demographic, socio- logical as well as technological factors.

▶ **The flaws of technologists**

There is a key flaw in the approach of technologists to their discussions of the future. They rarely question their own assumptions about the values of those for whom their technologies are intended. A major weakness in technologically-driven future scenarios is their failure to recognise that the world does not consist of masses of "undifferentiated" individuals. They ignore the significance of social structures, social institutions, cultures and values for shaping and nurturing similarities and diversities in lifestyles. But it is only through an understanding of these, and how they are likely to develop in the future, that it is possible to assess the take-up of new technologies and how these, in turn, will shape the future. The social science perspective is vital in assessing technological innovations and their impact on society. From this can emerge better informed debate and hopefully, policies for change. About what there is little doubt, however, is that ICTs will become more encompassing, inter- acting with social institutions to give individuals greater oppor- tunities and rewards in a future Britain that would be seen as science fiction but only a few years ago. They offer the capabilities of overcoming the age old issue of social and economic exclusion that has been so much a feature of Britain in the past. The challenge is whether there is the will and the determination by leaders in both the government and corporate sectors to realise the potential which these have to offer.

9

Commentary on the trends

▶ Carl Symon
▶ Jon Leach
▶ Robert M Worcester
▶ Michael Hughes
▶ Paul Edwards
▶ Heather Rabbatts

Commentary on the trends

▶ **Carl Symon**

Chairman and Chief Executive, IBM United Kingdom and Ireland

As I read this book, I was struck with how closely aspects of the opening scenarios resonate with those IBM is already discussing – and in some cases piloting – with our leading edge clients. Elements of this vision of 2010 are very much with us today from a technology point of view. And the real movers and shakers in all fields of business, education and government are those who are recognising this fact, and building strategies to capitalise on it. They are already adapting to the society of the 21st century. Britain in 2010 demonstrates, but perhaps should have emphasised even more, that information technology will increasingly pervade every aspect of life.

With the trend towards greater and greater individuality, choice and mobility, competitive advantage will depend on an organisation's ability to do completely personalised marketing, and to deliver completely personalised customer service. Customer service must be consistently available – where, when and how people want it. All the technology enablers to allow business to respond to this trend are in place. And the internet is at the heart of it all.

Our experience reflects, as indicated in the book, that he digital revolution is levelling the business playing field, especially for small to medium businesses. We have worked with very small businesses who have become global players through a Web presence which was developed in hours. They dramatically increased their sales, without having to invest in international offices. Now, growth is independent of physical presence. We relish this rise in entrepreneurship which the new technologies will help support, and which is predicted in this book.

A very significant trend which is implicit in the opening scenarios is the evolution of internet access into what we are calling Pervasive Computing. Web-based computing will be embedded in a very large number of devices – perhaps as many as a trillion. Today, we are at the early stages with intelligent mobile phones, smart cards and the beginnings of convergence of TV and the internet, but much more is to come. We are already demonstrating in-car sensors communicating with predictive maintenance systems, and "home of the future" where appliances and essential services are self-managed. There will be applications not yet thought of, embedded in the things people use in their everyday lives. As the technology continues to become significantly cheaper and more powerful, this trend will accelerate.

The evolution from today's personal computing to tomorrow's pervasive computing gives us confidence to predict a future which is more positive than the book's concerns about social exclusion. There are many, many ways in which technology will enable inclusion. Many organisations, institutions and governments already recognise that inclusion rests to a large degree on access to the internet which in turn will provide access to information, to services, to greater choice and to lower prices. Technology is an enabler here, not a barrier. This will increasingly be the case as more, low cost, easy to use devices become available. For example, as Digital TV and the internet converge, access to the vast knowledge resources of the web via everyday TV sets, TV games, consoles and set top boxes, will become a reality. There are strong indications that access devices will be bundled at little or no cost by the service or content provider, or the retailer, as illustrated by current trends in the digital TV market.

Technology has, and will continue to be, a powerful enabler of life long learning. Educational institutions will transform themselves as much as businesses will in the 21st century. Indeed, through IBM's Reinventing Education initiatives – the centrepiece of our global commitment to pre-university education – we are working with schools throughout the world to develop and implement innovative technology solutions designed to raise student attainment and modernise the management of education services. The IBM "Wired For Learning" Framework used in these partnerships promotes collaboration, and strengthens the links between home and the community.

The implications for government services delivery in the future are also significant. There is vast potential for IT to revolutionise government. A number of Governments across the world are already embracing this revolution, and providing a range of new services to their citizens over the internet. We welcome the steps taken here in the UK towards e-Government: this has to be the way forward for the e-Society of the future.

▶ **Jon Leach**

HHCL and Partners – Advertising Agency

If you're reading this you're in luck. Because it's probable that you are a well-educated, techno-literate, commercially sussed citizen poised to benefit hugely in the world of 2010 (as carefully described in this book). Hey, you wouldn't be reading this sort of stuff if you weren't part of the media-rati, the info-rati, or marketing-rati. So get ready to read about your wonderful new life.

To dumb down this book into a simple slogan we are about to enter a new type of society : Techno Feudalism. And you are the Media-age Mercenaries with all the freedom, wealth and adventure that comes with the job. Extrapolating from this book the Corporate Barons ("Big Business") will run the world. Government will be like a weak, irrelevant Monarch following the lead of the Barons. And the rest of the populace will consist of the dispossessed lowly paid Serfs (tilling the keyboards of their corporate masters) and the Media-age Mercenaries. The latter (i.e. you) will move flexibly from project to battle to project and be so valued for your creativity and knowledge that you will receive large sacks of gold from your so called superiors lurking behind their corporate firewalls. So richly will you be rewarded that you can take as much time off as you choose to play your lute and carouse in the tavern. Result. And in case you have a swarthy, muscular swordsman in your minds-eye, meet the new archetype for the Media-age Mercenary : she's female, she's single and she has an e-mail directory to die for.

(To be really precise she's called Rachel, she has a degree in "media studies and healthcare" and she runs her own advertising agency. One of the most compelling aspects of this book is the collection of scenarios where we read of a hypothetical individual's life.)

So how did we end up with Techno Feudalism? Projecting well established trends into the future, in a wired world of Hackers and Traders, national governments won't be able to control the flow of money and ideas. The global networked economy has set people free and there's no going back.

Unfortunately some people will be more free than others. So at one end of the scale the people and institutions that are motivated to accumulate wealth will continue to do so. Big Business will get bigger. It's human nature.

At the other end of the scale, the people excluded from this economy of ideas, creativity and communications (the non-surfing Serfs) will become even more excluded. Lacking in education, access to technology and suffering from the worst social problems, this book predicts that a large under-class will continue to exist. Even when working in front of a computer screen, if you're working in a call centre or a data entry factory you are likely to be underpaid, insecure and under-connected (already in 1999 you can be legitimately fired if caught using your company's net access for your personal use). Unfortunately in the age of Techno Feudalism the presence of a screen does not set you free. A horse can be used to carry you to many exciting new places or it can be yoked to a plough and pull you up and down a muddy field from dawn to dusk. So what of those lucky people in the middle? They are not a "Middle Class" but a "Mercenary Class". Educated, teched-up, confident in their ability to sell their services to the highest bidder (and pursue all their creative, balancing, spiritual interests as well). You lucky people! But there's a sting in the tale.

In the past Mercenaries have always been apolitical. They have chosen to operate outside normal society. They have no responsibility. But given the decline of Government influence, who is going to shape society? The serfs have no power. The Corporate Barons will continue to do what Barons have always done and pursue their own agendas.

Yes, the only people with any power to sway the Barons are you, the Media-age Mercenaries. Sorry, but in the age of Techno Feudalism you, gentle reader, will inherit "society". So from one Media-age Mercenary to another, a question: what are we going to do with it? A big question leading to a big, scary social programme, perhaps.

But like other 12 step recovery programmes, the first step is to decide if we are going to take responsibility for our own actions. It's fascinating to read about Rachel's intoxicatingly powerful position but what I want to know of our fictional 2010 advertising executive is will she take responsibility for her actions upon society as a whole?

So, Rachel (and my fellow media-age mercenaries) when our turn comes, when the Barons and the Serfs pause and wait for us to guide them into the next Techno Feudal era, I hope that we do the right thing. And make sure that it's better than the previous Feudal era.

▶ Robert M Worcester

Chairman, MORI

A Worrying Future Ahead? The speed of communications today means that more information, in both width and depth, is available to more people, faster, than ever before. The internet, mobile phones, pagers, laptops, scanners, modems, faxes, photocopiers and digital photography – most unknown 30 years ago – are all now widely available to ensure what one knows, we all know.

Knowledge is still power, as it always has been, but now increasingly in the hands of the many and not just the few. We all know the speed at which money travels today, and the implication that has for financial management and control. Information can travel at the same blinding speed.

The 20th Century has been called the "Measured Century", the first when economic, social, political and environmental conditions have been put to the discipline imposed by statistical systems, tracked over time, and the results distributed to both policymakers and more and more frequently to the people, mainly to the educated elites in the first half of the century, and in the latter, much more widely, both within countries and cross-nationally. The pace of change, corporate, product, political and consumer, is accelerating at an accelerating rate. To some people that is frightening all of the time, and to nearly everyone else it is frightening at least some of the time.

Longevity threatens economic stability, global movement and speed and independence of communications from government restrictions threatens economic sovereignty, the family structure is under threat, with the greatest projected growth the single person household, trends to the service economy and an increasing proportion of women in the workforce, downsizing and growth in part-time jobs, equally desired by both men and women, the rise of the civic society, rejection of role models and loss of confidence in institutions, acceptance of feminism and informality, loss of status and breaking down of hierarchies all present both threats and opportunities to our society.

Empirical data, and especially our work with the Socioconsult consortium of research companies across Europe, has identified a number of "cross-cultural convergences" to be taken into account:

▷ A growing gap between institutions and people
▷ A move from self-centredness to autonomy
▷ A flow from ideology to the need for more meaning to life
▷ A trend from an organised social structure to a network culture
▷ A current from feminism to feminisation of society
▷ A drift from rational to polysensorial.

All of these will affect our society.

Other convergences include

▷ Going from saving time to savouring time
▷ Going from pleasure-seeking to parallel crude and discerning hedonism
▷ Going from ecology to daily environmental friendliness

Britain is at the end of a long mutation; the society has basically transformed itself. The Thatcher revolution has run its course. Privatisation has reached its limits. We are on the "Third Way". But there is a growing sense that daily life has become too stressful, and that security is undermined. In the application of Maslow's "Hierarchy of Human Needs", sustenance is assured, but security is threatened. Esteem is under attack, and self-actualisation comes hard. Crude hedonism is on the rise; more drugs, and more anti-social behaviour, and growing faster with young women than young men; too many are what we call the "underwolves", which we define as the underdog who bites back.

In the rich world today there are three people in work to support one pensioner; by 2030, this ratio will fall to 1.5 to 1; most of the people reading this will be a pensioner then. It will take between 9 per cent and 16 per cent of the GDP in these countries to support today's pension promises, never mind the increased cost of health care and housing that will be required.

Now, pensioners represent one in five of the adult population, but one in four will be a pensioner in two decades. The typical retired household occupant in 20 years will be a lone woman.

All of this will result in resentments building up

▷ Young against old
▷ Poor against rich
▷ Rural against urban
▷ Scientists against the people
▷ Producers against consumers
▷ People against the Institutions
▷ Central government against local government
▷ Everybody against big business
▷ The Globalised (many) against the globalisers (few)

Engineers want high tech; people want high touch. The media are part of the problem, not part of the solution.

In light of these changing needs and wants, what does it mean when . . .

▷ The proportion – nearly half the workforce – who fear they are being left behind on IT skills has changed little over the last three years: 1996 – 46 per cent; 1997 – 45 per cent; 1998 – 47 per cent.

▷ One in five workers think that IT developments mean that they spend more time working now than two years ago.

There will be sceptics who will say that you can't take these things too seriously, that all that a company needs to do is to pile it high and sell it cheap, or build a better mousetrap and the world will beat a path to your door. It isn't like that these days, if indeed it ever was.

One person in six tell us they have boycotted a company's product on ethical grounds, and one in five that they have positively chosen a product or service because of a company's ethical reputation, and, eliminating the overlap between these two groups, because some have of course done both, some 38 per cent of the British public tell us that they have either done one or the other in that 12 months before our 1998 Corporate Social Responsibility Study.

Kermit the Frog reminds us "It ain't easy, being green". And the teachings of Abraham Maslow, who in 1943 taught the hierarchy of human needs, of sustenance, security, esteem and love, and then self-actualisation. Translated, I call this the Alligator Principle: when you're up to your neck in alligators, you don't worry a lot about global warming.

But government and society alike have to worry about global warming, and the environment generally, and corporate social responsibility, and human rights, and fair employment practices, and safety, and consumer rights, and, more. For it is society which gives the licence to government, to business, and to NGOs to do what they do, and they, increasingly, demand their right to decide whether to grant, or withhold, that licence.

▶ **Michael Hughes**

Director, Baring Asset Management

Experience has taught me that portfolio investment is more about direction than valuation. Financial markets' assessment of fair valuation changes over time. Identifying important turning points and hence new trends is more relevant.

Britain in 2010 identifies three trends which have relevance for financial markets. The first is the move towards single households; the second, the impact of new technologies; and the third, the consequences of globalisation.

Even if one was to question the assumption that single person households will account for almost 40 per cent of all households by 2010, the need for greater financial independence seems likely to grow. Governments are unlikely to meet the financial needs of an ageing population and changing employment practices will necessitate different savings arrangements.

Whatever foresight governments share with the electorate, it is highly likely that many people will be financially unprepared for retirement with the consequence that the effective retirement age for some may increase beyond current practice. Some, of course, may actively choose a second or even third career in order to combine quality of life with stimulation provided by work, and in preference to being economically inactive for twenty years or so. In all these circumstances, the role of savings could change. Savings may be for life (style) rather than just retirement.

Saving earlier in one's career than has previously been the norm allows a subsequent lifestyle to be subsidised. Such a choice can have consequences for the housing market. In high inflation times, new entrants became quick to take out a mortgage as soon as they had a paypacket. The lessons of how to survive and prosper in an inflationary economy were handed down from one generation to another. But will those now entering the workforce of a low inflation economy choose to rent rather than buy and save now to spend later? The incentives to save have rarely been greater. For most people it is possible to draw an income free of any tax on accumulated savings. This situation has been a long time coming, but is undoubtedly fair given that the decision to save is facilitated from income already subject to tax.

The challenge for the financial services industry is to provide lifetime savings products that are straightforward to use, provide an adequate level of risk taking and are not costly to administer. We have come a long way from using our first computer. Those of us of university age in the late sixties/early seventies have not so fond memories of preparing stacks of punched cards to be delivered to some distant computer. What then of the generation who becomes used to internet access through the home TV. The linking of existing home entertainment (i.e. TV and PC) to the outside world simply by plugging the telephone into the TV opens up a new dimension to living. But predicting what will then happen is much more difficult. Let me venture some ideas.

Since it will be much cheaper for companies to sell via the internet, there is an advantage in encouraging people to buy through this source. What greater advantage could there be than paying people to buy. Offering cash payments to use the internet carries important implications for companies which do not or who are slow to respond. internet access therefore becomes an increasingly important means of communicating with customers. From the customers' point of view the ease with which prices can be compared provides a potential gain to living standards not seen since the advent of electricity. This is very definitely the era of consumer empowerment. The consequences for corporate profitability are immense. The investment message is to avoid "torpedo" stocks –

those companies which are slow to respond to the challenges posed by new distribution channels.

Globalisation means many different things to different people. In the City it is normally equated with increasingly large capital flows and the ability to move money between markets. This can cause problems for governments who become concerned about tax avoidance and whose response is to shift more of the obligations of government onto the corporate sector. But they in turn are shifting the burden onto the individual via private pension and health arrangements, contracting out employment and restricting opportunities for advancement. This process can be destabilising for a society which comes to feel more uncertain about its future. Some, usually the higher paid, can take out insurance against unexpected developments. For most the prospects appear daunting. Reliance on state intervention may not be appropriate if the state is unable to raise sufficient taxation. And in a globally competitive environment governments are seeking to have the lowest marginal tax rates. One possible solution is for companies to pursue policies which promote stability by establishing foundations for supporting educational, health and community projects. Contributions made out of profits may be tax effective (governments could make them even more so) and help promote a corporate culture which may define an acceptable balance between capitalism and the distribution of resources in the twenty first century.

▶ **Paul Edwards**

Chief Executive, The Henley Centre

Esther Dyson, the new media analyst, tells a story in her book Release 2.0 of a party at Bill Gates' mansion. The house is wired in every conceivable way, but the centrepiece of the occasion was not digital but very analogue. The "celebrity glass blower" Dale Chihuly, with a

*team of assistants, set up shop on the balcony, in front of the guests,
and blew glass: craft as performance. "The magic was how real it was",
writes Dyson. "No electronics. No machines, even. Just people,
equipment, glass, the force of gravity, heat, and some shaping tools".*

The story is a reminder of how quickly even the new loses its value –
but an experience remains unique. A similar and surprisingly bad-
tempered argument has been raging about the future between the
economist Paul Krugman and Kevin Kelly, one of the leading
proponents of the wired world. Kelly's view, unsurprisingly, is that
the critical skills of the future will be those which exploit the
capabilities of the digital networked economy. Krugman suggests
instead that as computers and networks become smarter, their need
for human input will become smaller – and the humans needed in
this symbolic economy will have ever more arcane skills, dealing with
ever more abstract levels of meta-knowledge. The people whom
computers will not replace will be those who offer services and
experiences: gardeners, hairdressers, potters, glassblowers. Or perhaps more mundanely, telesales and customer service staff.

In practice, the outcome will probably be somewhere between the
two: it is implausible to hope that even the smartest computers will
rid us of the new priesthood of IT support staff, with their mystical
spells, acronymic incantations, and incomprehensible explanations.

But it is a useful reminder that while trends can help us imagine
the future (demographics have an air of inevitability about them)
others are merely signs pointing along one road that might be
travelled. They rarely tell the full story. Societies are complex and
adaptive systems, driven by millions of individuals with sophisticated
and apparently paradoxical behaviour.

For example, one of the forecasts which was commonplace during
the 1980s and much of the 1990s, and which became a policy driver
for the government, was that the number of cars in the UK would
double by 2020. The trend numbers had simply been extrapolated

forward a few years. No matter that it was difficult to conceive of where so many vehicles would be parked, or the congestion that would ensue, this was the basis for an aggressive policy of road-building. Recent research suggests that this was a self-fulfilling prophecy: that new roads encouraged cars on to the road for journeys which had been too inconvenient or had taken too much time by car before. The people who enjoy the convenience of the car are the same people who worry about their children getting asthma or being safe on the way to school: how such tensions play out are unpredictable. The emergence of transport during the summer of 1999 as a political issue is a sign of the kinds of conflicts which emerge as systems adjust. The outcomes are uncertain.

Similar realignments can be seen in the corporate sector. Depending on which figures one believes, anywhere between 50 per cent and 80 per cent of new value is generated from ideas. Downsizing and outsourcing, and the rise of contract employment, are now seen as increasingly at odds with the need to retain knowledge in the firm and to generate the intellectual capital that is now regarded as essential to the creation of this new value. A trend which seemed very clear during the 1980s is already provoking a response. Similar tensions can be seen in the rise in the number of single person households, soon to become the largest type of household. On the face of it, this may be the roots of a new mobile hedonism. Yet many of those single households are the products of divorced families, which face their own constraints in terms of money, time, and mobility.

Many of the current predictions of the future assume that the personal computer will be everywhere – or almost everywhere – by the year 2010. The sometime chief executive of the computer firm DEC, Ken Olsen, has been ridiculed for years for saying back in 1977 that he could see no reason for people to have PCs in their homes. Yet Olsen was right: his problem was that he did not predict the spread of the workplace into the home. The PC remains a complex and expensive device, and it is feasible that in its present form it is only a phase that we are going through: it will never break the 50 per cent barrier to become a mass consumer device. Even now in the United States internet penetration remains at less than a third. Meanwhile some of the early research suggests that children who are required to tote a laptop for lessons (as they are already at some exclusive New York schools) have – like management consultants – come to hate the burden they impose, whereas children at publicly-funded schools, with limited access, still regard them as a gateway to another world.

The impressions formed in youth stay with one for life. It is sometimes said that the old are not behaving as if they are old any more. More precisely, they are not behaving like the last generation of old people: they listen to Pink Floyd and the Rolling Stones and wear jeans, like they always have. Record companies and radio stations have discovered to their advantage that they will also listen to other bands who have listened to a lot of 60s music, such as Radiohead and Oasis. The current generation of fifty-year olds were shaped by a time in which choices were fewer but opportunities seemed richer, and those attitudes have stayed with them as they have grown older. Today's twenty-year olds worry about losing their jobs and having enough money for retirement. The future then, would seem to hold a bonanza for financial services companies which can talk to twenty-year olds without talking down to them. But in thirty years time, those same twenty-year olds are likely to be listening to dance music even while they are saving for the future.

The conservatism of these teenagers, which is a European, not just British phenomenon, is driven by wider concerns. Competition increases the range of choice, and sometimes drives down prices (with a nudge or two from a regulator). But choice is not universally appreciated. For some, especially those working longer hours, with less time, the range of choices is itself a source of anxiety. The Henley Centre's research suggests that less than a quarter of consumers have confidence that they will make the right decision when buying a complicated and expensive product such as a car, insurance, or other financial services.

This sense of being in and out of control is now so strong among consumers that it may, The Henley Centre believes, be undermining Maslow's "hierarchy of needs", one of the great certainties of the modern marketing profession. Maslow's model saw people moving up a ladder of needs as they became more affluent, leaving behind concerns over their physical surroundings and their security, seeking aesthetic experience and personal fulfilment. For thirty years it has been taken as a given that people no longer had to worry about the stuff at the bottom of the hierarchy and could concentrate on the profounder things in life. No more. Their insecurity over employment, money, and the instability of family life means that once more people are worrying about the basics.

This is a profound psychological shift, and we do not yet know how it will affect people's behaviour. Jonathan Storey has suggested recently that as the market forces itself into more and more areas of our lives, the resistance to this comes from our ancestral ghosts, the parts of our selves still connected to community, history, and place. For Bill Gates, this may take the form of celebrating ancient arts such as glass-blowing. For the rest of us, it could be a lot more disturbing.

▶ Heather Rabbatts

Former Chief Executive, London Borough of Lambeth

Those of us in public service are increasingly involved in trying to plan for uncertain futures. Assumptions made in the past are rapidly becoming obsolete as social trends overtake practice based on previous social models. So the changing nature of "community", the rise in single parent households, the globalisation effect, access to instant information and hence power, the gap between the information rich and information poor are all features of this new landscape.

The social trends data gathered here helps those of us involved in public service to begin to think outside the box and imagine the futures in which our services and communities will be based. A striking theme emerging is the rate and pace of change are of such an order that organisationally we need to ensure that we plan and structure ourselves on a "scenario" basis rather than trying to have an inflexible long-term strategy. Some commentators currently argue that this change process is one that is akin to the social ramifications which the industrial revolution brought in its wake.

It would be a sign of real failure if bureaucracies and large corporations failed to grasp this and so fail to provide the right kind of service support and infrastructure that future generations will require.

For those in public service, defined in its broadest terms, the changing role of community and its psychological importance have particular resonance.

The word community conjures up an image of homogeneity, geography, location and identity. Yet in London the reality of community is of a very different ilk to the image conjured up by the phraseology. Community is increasingly defined via complex net-works which are fluid and spatial and may be defined by "interests" rather than historical allegiance. The sense of place and home is constantly shifting and what is today's community of interest is not necessarily tomorrow's.

How services are orchestrated across this complex web will be different and will have a major impact on organisational design and corporate governance. How democracy is enriched and public servants trusted in this environment, especially where authority is constantly subject to question, will be a major challenge.

The jury is obviously still out in terms of whether the new

democratic structures breathe life back into citizens and the notion of active participation. In the world of joined up thinking and action the power of IT and instant communications still remain under-exploited. For example, those of us seeking to pull together the idea of life-long learning and turning the vision into operational reality we are at the dawn of virtual classrooms, universities and places of learning. Soon it will be possible to truly create classrooms without walls. This leap of imagination requires us in the public sector to throw off some of the structures of the past and begin to create radical new models. If someone can undertake a degree course which has the best from higher education in this country, the USA, Europe and the Far East at their fingertips in their home, office, community centre, by global teaching by the best educators in the world, the higher education structure will look radically different the quality of learning will be a quantum leap from where we are currently. The data here begins to provoke our imagination, to think the unthinkable, to create, innovate and to provide the bridges from exclusion to inclusion.

Index

About Foresight

Foresight is about using knowledge of what the future might hold to identify what could happen and turn it to advantage. It is not about predicting the future, but rather about being alive to what could happen ten or twenty years ahead and building that knowledge into current thinking and decision making. About looking beyond past experience and simple extrapolation of what is happening here and now and recognising that the future will be different – radically different – from what has gone before.

The UK Foresight Programme was launched by the Government in 1994 to provide a basis for building sustained, national long-term competitive advantage and improving quality of life by

▷ identifying market drivers, threats and opportunities beyond normal commercial time horizons and informing decisions taken today;

▷ building bridges between science and business – getting people who understand the possibilities opened up by advances in science and technology to communicate effectively with people who understand consumer needs and requirements;

▷ pooling knowledge and expertise – within sectors and across sectoral and disciplinary boundaries – to increase national prosperity and well being.

The Programme is currently spear-headed by 13 Panels, mostly business led and drawn from business, the science base, the voluntary sector and government. Some Panels focus on specific industries whilst others are relevant to many different sectors. In addition, there is a wide and growing range of Associate Programmes – Foresight projects which are being carried out by Research Councils, professional bodies, trade associations and other organisations with relevant knowledge and expertise.

Sectoral Panels	Thematic Panels
▷ Built Environment and Transport	▷ Ageing Population
▷ Chemicals	▷ Crime Prevention
▷ Defence, Aerospace and Systems	▷ Manufacturing 2020
▷ Energy and Natural Environment	
▷ Financial Services	Every panel is asked to consider education, skills and training issues and the implications of its proposals for sustainable development.
▷ Food Chain and Crops for Industry	
▷ Healthcare	
▷ Information, Communications and Media	
▷ Materials	
▷ Retail and Consumer Services	

Each of the Panels has published work plans for the period up to November 2000. The Programme as a whole will continue at least to March 2004.

'Britain Towards 2010' was produced by Foresight to stimulate details about the implications of possible social futures and help to underpin the work of the 13 Panels. Many of the issues it identifies are being considered by Panels in more detail. For example:

▷ the Ageing Population Panel is looking at the impact of changes in demographic structure on markets and social structures;
▷ the Manufacturing 2020 Panel is looking at the key issues which will shape long term manufacturing in the UK;
▷ the Crime Prevention Panel is looking at the implications of new technology for crime and the prevention of crime and at how changes in social trends and structures will shape both the nature of crime and the role of technology in increasing or reducing it;
▷ the Retail and Consumer Services Panel is looking at scenarios for the growth of personal e-commerce;
▷ the Information, Communications and Media Panel is looking at the learning process in 2020 and the potential impact of technology on schools and what and how children are taught.

Panels will be putting their initial ideas and proposals out to consultation in the first half of 2000. The aim is to ensure that people with knowledge and expertise to offer have the opportunity to contribute to the development of Panel thinking and formulation of recommendations for action, and more generally to stimulate thinking about the future. Anyone who wishes to contribute is welcome to do so. Since Foresight is fundamentally about shaping their future, special efforts are being made to involve young people and give them the opportunity to feed in their views

One of the main channels for communication will be the Foresight Knowledge Pool at **www.foresight.gov.uk** which has full, up-to-date information about Panel activities. The Pool contains all the outputs from the UK Programme to date and Foresight reports produced by other organisations. It also provides single point access to a wide range of data and views on the future from the UK and overseas; information about regional Foresight activity; and information about how you can apply the Foresight process to your own organisation or business.

Alternatively, fax the Foresight team on 020 7215 6715, tell them what you would like to know more about and they will do their best to help.